# There is Another Way to Happiness

*The Four Step CAST Process that Will Transform Your Life*

**Ski Chilton, PhD**

**with Josh Chilton**

There Is Another Way to Happiness: The Four Step CAST Process That Will Transform Your Life



ISBN: 978-1-950336-41-8

Published by Authors on Mission

This book is for informational and entertainment purposes only. This book is not meant to be used, nor should it be used, to diagnose or treat any medical condition. For diagnosis or treatment of any medical, emotional, or psychological problem, consult your own physician or counselor.

In loving memory of my dear parents, Ruby and Floyd (FH), who departed from this Earth far too soon. Their enduring guidance continues to daily illuminate my path from beyond.

# Table of Contents

# Introduction

Almost a decade ago, I settled into a corner office in the newly built Biotech Place at Wake Forest Innovation Quarter. During this time, an encounter in the hallway shook me to my core. My department chair had asked me to introduce myself to a group of European visiting scientists and students. As I toured them through my pristine lab and introduced them to my research team, I couldn't help but share my usual tale of triumph over adversity. It was a story I had told countless times before—an account of overcoming great obstacles, born as a severely dyslexic child on a humble tobacco farm in rural Appalachia. With hard work and determination, I rose to prestigious positions at institutions like Johns Hopkins and Wake Forest School of Medicine. I concluded my story by highlighting my three decades of scientific research, including numerous publications, books, and accolades.

However, as I spoke, I sensed a duality within myself. I began to realize that two entities were vying for my attention: First, there was my "Me," my egoic self, who was doing all the talking and boasting, but also another, an "I", a seeming Observer, that appeared to be a part of me simply witnessing the unfolding events. Listening to "Me" that day, my "I" seemed to be projecting a deep sense of discomfort and sadness at my own arrogance. "I" was appalled by the elaborate performance the egoic part of my being had perfected over the years. The story I told was a concoction of facts, exaggerations, and half-truths—a mythical narrative about an academic hero battling dragons and making groundbreaking discoveries to save the world from medical disasters and ignorance. The more my Observer heard, the greater the discordance between actual facts, exaggerations, and half-truths. At that moment, "I" decided to stop telling that story in that hallway.

“I apologize,” I said, interrupting myself. “Let's start over. Everything I just shared with you was a mythical tale—a blend of facts, exaggerations, and half-truths.” Mark Twain once said, “A half-truth is the most cowardly of lies.” At that moment, I realized I had been narrating a cowardly story, and the coward was “Me”. I imagined those visiting scientists and students probably thinking, “This poor man is having a mental breakdown.” Perhaps I was losing my mind. I would later discover that losing that “Me” was not necessarily a negative thing. In fact, escaping the dominance of my “Me” would become my path to finding freedom, love, and peace and discovering the innate happiness within me that had been hidden all along.

That incident in the hallway was not the only existential crisis I faced at that point in my life. The inconsistencies between my desired actions and my conditioned responses plagued me. I wanted to do good and be kind, yet there was something deep within “Me” that reflectively reacted to the past, causing “Me” to act in ways that hurt those I loved the most. That isolated part of “Me” had been destructive in two failed marriages. I relied on multiple prescription medications, battled cancer, and felt isolated. I had become a hypersensitive, resentful, angry, and fearful man. My obsession with professional achievements—grants, papers, books, and promotions—was an attempt to find fleeting joy and excitement. My mind was filled with fear-based narratives, constantly fixated on problems, dramas, and tragedies. This “Me” was highly insecure, convinced that people were dismissing or taking advantage of him while believing he held the ultimate truth. Worst of all, my mind would loop endlessly, ruminating on all these thoughts day and night.

I am eternally grateful for that moment in the lab hallway where I first recognized my Observer (my conscious Self), who was clearly aware of the half-truths and falsehoods perpetuated by the boastful, loud-mouthed “Me.” This unsettling experience marked the beginning of my awakening. Over the next few years, I would learn a great deal about my adult and childhood conditioning, my ‘shadow’, the egoic self, and how they all played a critical role in my autopilot reactionary state. Above all, these early events made me aware that the person I pretended to be was inconsistent with who I wanted to be and who I was meant to be. It was a profound existential crisis, with conflicting emotions, ruminations, reactions, and moments of awareness battling against my painful and angry feelings. I recognized that my emotional reactions, especially in my personal life, continued to ignite metaphorical fires that consumed me, my relationships, my well-being, and most of all, my happiness.

It would be several years before I would discover that one of my most admired spiritual teachers, Eckhart Tolle, had experienced a similar 'inner transformation' at age 29. Like me, he endured extended periods of depression. He was awakened one night from his sleep to two separate entities within him, after years of suffering from feelings that were "almost unbearable." At that moment, he suddenly underwent a similar confusing, terrifying, but life-changing spiritual experience. By the following morning, he was filled with a sense of "uninterrupted deep peace and bliss" that has never left him since. Later, as he walked around, he marveled at the miracle of life on Earth, as if he had just been born. He went on to write influential spiritual books like *The Power of Now*[1], *Stillness Speaks*[2], and *A New Earth*[3]

My journey, however, did not unfold as rapidly as Tolle's. I didn't experience a permanent life-altering transformation overnight. So, I delved deeper. I initially took a more academic path, questioning whether humans, including myself, truly possessed free will. Given the chaos in our minds, could our behaviors, actions, and thoughts be altered, or were they predetermined to be controlled by our life conditioning and evolutionary programming? Most importantly, could I escape this toxic inner drama and duality, or was I condemned to manage it and suffer its consequences?

If we experience this constant duality—the egoic self alongside the conscious Self, or the "Me" and the "I"— then how does free will work, if at all? To confront this question of free will, I turned to the only approach I knew: objectivity, empiricism, and logic. I enrolled in the

Wake Forest School of Divinity for a semester and spent a year studying the concept of free will under a scholar trained at Princeton and Yale. I hoped to find answers by examining the works of great thinkers—from Aristotle and Augustine to Chisholm and Kane. While this intellectual and philosophical exploration fascinated me, I discovered that even the greatest minds couldn't agree on this subject. If they couldn't find the answers, how could I?

One area particularly intrigued me during this deep dive into free will. It was the concept of dual-process reasoning, where in our brains, one process operates rapidly, automatically, and unconsciously while the other is slower, deliberative, and conscious. I found the pioneering work of Jonathan Evans captivating, as he described humans as having "two minds in one brain" that compete for control over thoughts and actions[4]. This resonated deeply with my personal experience.

Remember that moment in the hallway where I introduced myself? That was the rapid, automatic, unconscious "Me" in action. Evolutionary biologists have long recognized the presence of a primitive "lizard" brain in the brainstem, cerebellum, and temporal lobes just behind the complex "human" brain in the frontal cortex layers. We tend to react to events, especially stressful ones, from the bottom up—the lizard brain takes charge first. It's equipped with instincts, rapid associations, and automatic control, leaving us little say in the matter. No wonder the boastful "Me" couldn't keep quiet. It was instinctively compelled to focus on my evolutionary, experiential, and societal programming centered on fear, competition, and past and future events. The lizard brain naturally reacts with exaggerated stories and half-truths produced from unconscious emotions designed to warn us about everything that could go wrong while fueling our egos to ensure the survival of our "precious genes." In general, this part of the brain could care less if I'm happy; it simply wants me to be on edge and ready to strike.

On the other hand, the modern human brain, our frontal cortex, emerged relatively recently, about 100,000 years ago. It differs from the unconscious lizard brain in nearly every aspect. The modern mind, housing the "I," is contemplative, capable of weighing decisions by simulating future outcomes. However, unlike the unconscious mind, it is slow and deliberate, taking its time before reaching a verdict. Science and my own experience aligned, confirming the ongoing battle within my mind, with the emotionally hyper-reactive lizard brain prevailing time and again, insuring there would be no peace or joy.

I was so captivated by this model of mind duality that in 2016, I wrote a book titled *The Rewired Brain*[5], exploring the existence of two competing minds and how they give rise to unconscious and conscious feelings, reactions, and decisions. In the book, I emphasized how certain fears and instincts rooted in our ancient evolutionary and lifetime programing continue to control us, causing emotional dysfunction. I offered deliberate processes to alter brain connectivity and improve our lives by changing our conscious thoughts and overriding our unconscious narratives. I felt it was a significant step forward, as it brought awareness to the source of much of my pain and the pain experienced by humanity. Yet, it wasn't enough. Something was still missing.

The inadequacy of my book became apparent during a small book signing at Barnes and Noble. A candid woman approached me, visibly frustrated, and said, "I'm mad at you! You described why I messed up my life, but you didn't provide a solution. Sure, you gave some tips and exercises to explore my true Self, but they weren't really all that helpful." Her words stung, for they revealed a truth—I had provided an analysis of the problem but failed to offer effective solutions. She said, "The book was like describing a tumor without providing the means to cure it." Ouch! I had attempted to give people an understanding of why we react destructively, but I hadn't given them the tools to change. To be honest, at the time, I had not yet discovered the solution myself.

In the winter of 2017, feeling discouraged by my lack of answers, I returned to the drawing board. My academic nature clung to the scientific literature, seeking guidance. I was aware of eastern spiritual practices like meditation and their integration into Western medicine, thanks to pioneers like Jon Kabat-Zinn in the 1970s. But I had no idea of the remarkable progress made in demonstrating the positive effects of these practices on emotional processing and stress management. I delved into research examining mindfulness meditation's impact on physical and mental conditions like depression, anxiety, PTSD, inflammation, and chronic pain. I was astounded. In 2000, a search of the term "meditation" in scientific literature yielded only 70 papers. Today, over 9,600 scientific papers with over 300 clinical trials have been published.

Many modern meditation practices have their roots in Buddhism, spanning 2,600 years. These practices emphasize maintaining attention and awareness of emotions, thoughts, feelings, and sensations while approaching them with openness, acceptance, compassion, and surrender. I realized that meditation cultivated the qualities I had attributed to the Observer long before I understood anything about meditation.

Almost six years ago, I began meditating. I had no idea what I was doing, but I used a meditation app called "Insight Timer" to explore guided meditations that resonated with me and my newfound Observer. In the first few months, quieting my lizard brain for even a few minutes was challenging. My attention darted from thought to thought as if I were in a storm-tossed boat in rough waters. But I persisted, and slowly, over time, my meditation practice deepened. I discovered that the more I allowed my thoughts to come and go without attachment or judgment, the calmer my mind became. I was training my brain to witness the thoughts and emotions rather than becoming entangled in them.

Five years ago, I was recruited to the University of Arizona in Tucson to build a Center for Precision Nutrition and Wellness. I was feeling pretty good about myself living in a city that was a southwestern center of wellness while I continued to gain confidence in my meditation practice. In fact, my lizard brain was so proud of me that he did everything he could to convince me that in a short amount of time, I had already become a mindfulness master, a Buddhist monk of sorts. I didn't realize that as I became more impressed with my newly acquired mindfulness, I was placing myself at great risk of losing it.

My wife's love for horses had brought two magnificent Arabians into our lives; one which we had rescued had endured a harrowing past of neglect and abuse. This majestic creature, a 5-year-old, recently gelded stallion, possessed an untamed spirit that challenged my ego. By taming the wild horse, I was determined to prove my mettle as a North Carolina redneck cowboy. With unyielding confidence, I believed I could train this magnificent beast; however, its untamed strength was no match for my resolute will. Even after writing *The Rewired Brain*[5], somehow, I did not realize that this audacious boast was merely the echo of my lizard brain, my primitive programing now clouding my judgment. The weight of my arrogance was soon to be reckoned with.

In a Sunday morning violent encounter, the horse nearly killed me, fracturing my pelvis in half and shattering my illusions. Unconscious and broken, I awakened in a hospital room, greeted by an orthopedic surgeon who delivered the bittersweet news. I was fortunate to be alive, yet the fractured pieces of my pelvis would require an intricate network of rods and bolts to restore functionality. As I recovered, the voices within grew louder, tormenting me with self-doubt and blame. The lizard brain shouted at me about what an idiot and loser I was and how I would never walk or be intimate with my wife again. It was telling me how I was really the victim here, and this whole thing was my wife's, my dumb cowboy friend's, and God's fault. As the inner turmoil and physical pain became too much to bear, I sought solace in daily meditation, unaware at the time that profound awakenings lay ahead.

I had no idea whether "I" and my burgeoning conscious awareness could evolve to meet this moment. I decided to go outside each morning at 5:30 a.m. in my wheelchair and sit in front of a beautiful, majestic palm tree I called "Divine Presence." With each sunrise, I would sit in stillness, cultivating a meditative space where answers might emerge. The furious voices within initially grew louder, drowning out the serenity, but within that chaos, I discovered the power of awareness. I learned to observe without attachment, to release the grip of anger, self-loathing, and fear.

Moreover, I understood the perils of allowing these destructive emotions to persist, for they produced the very inflammation that impeded my physical recovery.

Through weeks of unwavering dedication, a subtle shift began to occur, and this change was different than I expected from my scientific understanding of the human conscious and unconscious minds. The Observer within me appeared to be mystically transformed into a Healer—a conduit through which pain could be acknowledged, accepted, and surrendered to. Rather than evading discomfort, I confronted it head-on, embracing it within my awareness. And as the weeks unfolded, the shackles of pain relinquished their grip, replaced by newfound strength. Today, as I write these words, I stand as a testament to the miraculous power of the Observer and Healer within, eventually completely healing physically from the accident.

Yet, my journey did not cease with physical restoration. The Observer beckoned me deeper, urging me to explore the vines from past experiences and programing that continued to manifest as persistent thoughts and emotions. With unwavering curiosity, "I" journeyed into the recesses of my being, uncovering the layers of pain, conditioning, and trauma that had long shaped my perception of who Ski Chilton was. The Observer started assuming other transcendent roles, such as Counselor, Forgiver, and Divine Creator, and It guided me through the maze of my own consciousness.

With continued practice over the next year, my transformation became tangible. I began to experience moments of pure presence and stillness—glimpses of a profound peace that surpassed any fleeting pleasure or achievement. My relationships improved as my reactivity lessened, and I became more present and attentive to my loved ones. I discovered that the solutions to my problems lay not in the stories and dramas of the past or future but in the stillness of the present moment—the only place where life truly unfolds.

As I reflected on my odyssey, I began to recognize that my awakening from the depths of unconsciousness to the expanses of conscious living had occurred in four beautiful, overlapping steps. Importantly, completing one step was a necessary step that allowed me to progress to the next step. I could not believe the marvelous spiritual insight that traversing to the summit of each step provided and how, collectively, this path had completely transformed me. First, I awakened to the boundless **C**onsciousness that I now call my "I", recognizing it as the consistent essence of my being and the guide to uncover my innate happiness. Second, I expanded my **A**wareness, unearthing the unconscious beliefs, conditioning, trauma, instincts, and patterns that had kept me imprisoned for far too long. Third, I embraced the transformative power of acceptance and **S**urrender, relinquishing my illusions of control, especially under the most difficult circumstances. Fourth, I nurtured my **T**rust, faith, and confidence in universal intelligence and creativity that weaves its tapestry through all existence, knowing that it guides and supports me not only in this short-lived life but throughout eternity.

Dear reader, within the depths of these pages lies a gateway to your own mystical adventure—a path that unveils your "I", your true Self, and connects you with the Divine presence that resides within. My journey has been shaped not by conventional notions of success but by the alignment of curiosity, resilience, and an aversion to emotional pain. These attributes have propelled me to seek answers in the tangible world of science and within the boundless realms of subjective experience.

Within the ten chapters and thirteen weeks of mindful/meditation practices that follow, I will guide you through the CAST Process along a sacred path of profound self-discovery, sharing the wisdom and insights gleaned from my own life's adventure. I am humbled and grateful that you have chosen to accompany me on this voyage. Together, let us embark on this transformative journey. It is within our reach to navigate the depths of consciousness, choose love and forgiveness, and discover that *There is Another Way to Happiness*.

# Step 1 –

# Awakening to Consciousness

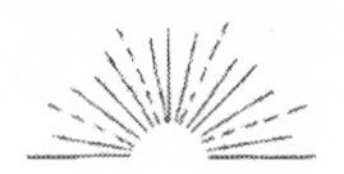

When we lose touch with the innermost essence of our being, the profound "I Am" that resides within us, we find ourselves ensnared in the tortuous world of false beliefs spun by our unconscious mind, attachments, current circumstances, fears, and the deep imprints of our childhood and societal conditioning. This illusory, cunning, and treacherous realm becomes a nightmarish landscape that breeds unhappiness, confusion, heartache, and a profound sense of loneliness. It can also perpetuate cycles of cruelty, causing us to unwittingly inflict pain upon others.

Within the pages of this book, spirituality takes center stage—a grand odyssey of awakening from the slumber of our existence to unlock realms of pure consciousness. Regrettably, most of us remain blissfully unaware of their dormant state. We enter this world in a state of unconsciousness, traverse through life in a state of obliviousness, form connections and build families while still immersed in their lifelessness, and ultimately depart from this realm without ever truly rousing from our deep sleep. This profound lack of awareness typically permeates our entire existence, casting a veil over our true potential to love ourselves and the world.

In light of this reality, it is little wonder that the concept of "dying to the self" holds profound significance across numerous religious traditions, including mine. My interpretation of this concept lies in the metaphorical demise of our 'shadow' selves, the conditioned and unconscious aspects of our being. Only by shedding these layers of conditioned existence can we glean a profound understanding of the splendor and magnificence inherently woven into the tapestry of human life. Through this transformative process, we transcend the confines of ordinary existence and embark upon a sacred pilgrimage toward unconditional love and the Divine.

The chapters within Part 1 - Awakening **C**onsciousness are purposefully crafted to jolt the reader out of this lifeless state, presenting nourishing hope that transcending the 'shadow' self and the confines of conditioned existence is indeed possible. They beckon us to break free from the prison in which we have unwittingly entrapped ourselves, to embrace liberating true choice, and to excavate the depths of our authentic Selves, our "I". These chapters serve as the vital steppingstones for the remainder of the book, propelling us forward on our spiritual journey, unveiling self-knowledge, and guiding us towards a profound encounter with the boundless and untapped realms of the true Self and the Divine.

# Chapter 1-

# Who is *I*?

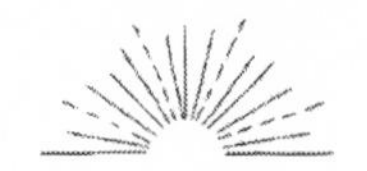

## Quest for Happiness

This book is about a quest for happiness, a journey through life's brutal truths, and the transformational power of our struggles. It's about awakening to the fact that a more beautiful path to happiness exists, often only discovered when we've been pummeled enough by emotional and relational challenges. The wisdom offered here isn't from a psychologist, psychiatrist, or spiritual guru but from someone whose insights are rooted in evolutionary biology and inspired by painful personal experiences and mindful teachings from history's greatest minds.

I seek to guide us, not through defining truths but by shedding light on our barriers to happiness. I have come to believe that true self-discovery comes not from identifying who we are but by unearthing who we are not, by peeling away the layers of fears, roles, and attachments that mask our true Selves. I don't pretend to define God or the Divine because I don't believe I or anyone can truly understand the miracles all around us. I believe anyone who professes otherwise is likely spiritually arrogant and lost. But I hope to help us navigate the misconceptions that ensnare us, hoping we can gradually let them go and sense the Creative

Intelligence (the Divine) and beauty that surrounds us.

This book will undoubtedly challenge ingrained beliefs and concepts about life that drive collective unhappiness. The goal is to unlearn and dismantle the conditioning and attachments that cause our discontent. These are especially prevalent in Western societies. I propose that genuine happiness can only be found by questioning and relinquishing our conditioning, roles, and attachments. You might find your reactions ranging from surprise to annoyance as you read this book. You may strongly disagree or even consider me a lunatic, but that's alright. If you approach these pages with an open mind, ready for discovery, I believe there is a good chance that you will find exactly what you're searching for.

A central inference of the book is that what we seek, happiness, peace, and love already exist within us. If the goal is to awaken, we must let go of our preconceived notions and ingrained beliefs. In truth, most of us don't really want unqualified happiness if it means surrendering our need for control. Our version of happiness is typically conditional: "I'd be happy if I have this and that... if I can hold onto my attachments." We can't fathom the idea of contentment without these stipulations because they form the basis of our conditioning. However, if we aspire for genuine freedom and resulting happiness, we must shed these demands. These are the prison walls we have built around ourselves to incarcerate and isolate us from happiness. The central question this book poses is, are you willing to exchange control – the source of so much strain, ill-health, emotional turmoil, fear, conflicts, and confusion in your life – for a different approach? Are you willing to try another way?

The lynchpin of this entire journey will be self-observation and mindfulness. Let's start this process right now with a simple exercise. Pause for a moment right where you are and pay attention to your thoughts as you read this book. Note your bodily sensations, the activities of your mind, your emotional state. If you're having a reaction to the book, at least be aware that you are having the reaction. Be conscious of your presence in the room – say to yourself, "I'm in this room." Try observing yourself as if you were someone else, looking at yourself and sensing your thoughts.

Both in science and spirituality, I firmly believe in the concept of 'first principles.' The concept of 'first principles' refers to the foundational truths upon which complex ideas are built. In science, first principles, like Newton's laws of motion or Einstein's theory of relativity, form the basis that gives rise to entire fields of study. This approach encourages us to dissect problems to their simplest forms, challenge assumptions, and rebuild understanding from the bottom up, promoting innovation. In spirituality, first principles reflect fundamental spiritual truths, such as the existence of a higher level of consciousness. They help us strip away dogmas or inherited concepts, allowing us to reconstruct personalized, authentic spiritual understandings and frameworks.

In spirituality and waking up to true happiness, I believe the first and most important principle is discovering who we truly are, our true Self. This is opposed to the identities that society, our programming, and early childhood experiences have thrust upon us.

We must begin with questions such as, where does happiness dwell within my being - where does it originate? How am I connected to other beings, higher levels of consciousness, or the Divine? I deeply believe that once we have identified our true Self, we can discover happiness within us.

**A Hidden Masterpiece**

So, let's set off on this mystical journey with one question, the first principle that means the most. Who is "I"? Plato, more than two millennia ago, posited a thought experiment to shine a light on this quandary. Let's revisit this age-old analogy[6]. Picture yourself on an early Mediterranean morning, standing on a tranquil beach. The sea is serene, the sky a brilliant blue.

You decide to dive into the water to explore the underwater wonders – the vibrant fish, intriguing shells, and patterned sandy bed. Then, something large, dark, and formless on the seabed grabs your attention.

With effort, you manage to haul it ashore. It's covered in centuries-old accumulation of slime, crustaceans, seaweed, and shells – a grotesque, hardened mass. But as you painstakingly remove the debris, you uncover a stunning statue of a sea-god chiseled in brilliant marble by an exceptionally skilled sculptor. What initially appeared as a shapeless heap was concealing a timeless masterpiece of beauty.

This, to me, symbolizes our pristine and beautiful true Self, our forgotten essence. Plato likened the soul underneath to the statue of the divine Glaucus. In Greek mythology, Glaucus was a sea-god, born mortal and then turned immortal. It was believed that he came to the rescue of sailors and fishermen in storms.

So, we are like an exquisite piece of marble, lost at the bottom of the sea, its grandeur hidden under the accumulated sediment of our conditioning. Over time, this Divine statue, the masterpiece that is us, takes on the grotesque appearance of a monster. Yet, beneath the surface, we remain. No matter where we are in life, we remain beautiful underneath. This is us, who our "I" is, the very core of our true authentic Self. Unfortunately, this sacred place lies forgotten in the recesses of our unconscious, buried under the debris of frustrations, memories, fear-ridden images, and childhood traumas.

What I find most encouraging about this analogy is that recovery is possible. We can rediscover our beautiful statue, cleanse it, and restore its original magnificence. We can reconnect with the timeless aspect of our being – free from ties, memory, roles, or responsibilities. Below it all, we are a magnificent Self that transcends our identities – not a man or woman, old or young, rich or poor.

## We Are Not Our Roles

It wasn't until 2005, while drafting a biographical snippet for the press kit of my book *Inflammation Nation*[7], that I began to see the accumulation of slime, crustaceans, seaweed, and shells that had hidden my beautiful Self. It's not what you think. Over ten pages of writing the story of my life, a realization crystallized: I hadn't pursued this relentless path of success for the love of science or the joy of discovery. No, fear – fear of failure, fueled by a profound sense of unworthiness – had driven me all along.

Now, you might be wondering, where did this sense of worthlessness come from? How could it possibly plague someone as successful as you?

I was born and raised in an impoverished corner of the South, nestled at the foot of the Appalachian Mountains. The days of my early childhood were consumed by ceaseless work on our eight-acre tobacco farm and looking after our hog, our only guarantee of meat for the winter. My uncorrectable vision and severe dyslexia in the early years made learning almost impossible. In the rural North Carolina community of the late 60s and 70s, where I grew up, school took a backseat to farm work and sports. Reading, writing, arithmetic – they were simply not a priority. So, nobody noticed my struggle with dyslexia. In the eyes of my teachers, I was, and I hate to use this word, "retarded".

During my sixth and seventh grades, I was exiled to a small white building away from the main school. It was a limbo of sorts, a holding pen for children with various challenges – from severe intellectual disabilities to dyslexia and behavioral issues – all of us lumped together without much thought. There, education gave way to stress and anxiety, while my self-esteem was ground into dust.

Labels were cruel and blatant. The "A" class was for the smart ones, "B" for the slightly above average, "C" for those who were not so bright, and "D", my class, was the domain of the leftovers. The scorn wasn't hidden, and neither was the message: I was nothing more than a "retarded boy in the little white building."

Everyone always wants to know how I escaped that little white building. Funny enough, my first IQ test at the beginning of eighth grade set me free. I did surprisingly well and was whisked off to the "A" class. But the damage was done, and the insecurities and fear of not being good enough lingered. I still couldn't read and really would not efficiently learn to until after high school. In fact, given the verbal score on my SAT, the only way I got into college was that I was a good athlete, and they needed a pole vaulter on the track team. However, even with that, I couldn't shake off the feeling that everyone wanted me back in that "D" class, and metaphorically, there would always be this monstrous woman chasing me, trying to put me back into that little white building. These experiences and childhood trauma deeply scarred me, so deeply that I still feel them today.

So, I turned to work as a salve for the raw wounds of my unworthiness felt in childhood. Biology, biochemistry, genetics, and evolution became my sanctuaries in college. I threw myself into research, setting records, and publishing papers. I finished a five-year Ph.D. in three, worked with one of the country's most esteemed scientists, and joined the faculty at Johns Hopkins, rapidly moving through the academic ranks. My pain fueled my snowballing ambition, but every achievement only made me desperately crave the next one.

Meanwhile, as described in the Introduction, my personal life was unraveling. Despite having a lovely wife and four wonderful children, my relentless 16-hour workdays took a toll. My marriage crumbled, my father passed away, and I was given a couple of cancer diagnoses that felt like death sentences.

I achieved so much by societal standards, yet I was drowning in despair. Despite my long list of accomplishments, I was not enough. My life was a cocktail of unhappiness, anger, frustration, fear, and depression, stirred daily by a deadening mix of blood pressure, anti-depression, and anxiety medications. My forty-page-plus CV served as a reminder of my external accomplishments, but internally, I was spiraling. The joy of each new peak was fleeting, swiftly replaced by a familiar void. Each success was a brief flash of light, soon swallowed by the dark clouds of my chronic depression. It became so unbearable that I even toyed with the idea of ending it all.

So, what about the advice in all those top-notch self-help business and success books that flew off the shelves like hotcakes and became some of the best-selling books of all time. Books such as *Think and Grow Rich*,

*Rich Dad, Poor Dad*, *Seven Habits of Highly Effective People,* and that oldie but goodie, *How to Win Friends and Influence People*. I may not have followed their exact prescriptions, but certainly ended up where they and all Western societies said I should have.

In the Bible, Solomon, the author of Ecclesiastes, poignantly describes this as "Vanity of vanities" (1:2) – a fleeting vapor that appears one moment and disappears the next. By the time I turned forty-five, life had imparted a stark truth: the conventional markers of success – the material possessions, the accolades, the accomplishments, the startup companies, the status – are just ephemeral distractions. It was becoming clear that they could not quench my deepest thirsts or soothe my most profound pains. And there I was, imprisoned by my own ego, chained to my past, and yearning for an elusive sense of worth.

The struggle of self-discovery and finding another way is a steep and lonely climb, a maze of self-doubt and fear. However, through the fog of unworthiness and the echoes of past pains, there lies an opportunity to confront our inner demons, our childhood conditioning, to learn, and to rebuild. I kept asking if I am not my roles (including a world-class scientist, author, serial entrepreneur, and even more fundamental, a father), then who the hell am I? Somehow, I sensed deep inside my being that somewhere underneath this "greatest of mysteries" lay a path to happiness and peace that did not depend on anything, especially my accomplishments. Underneath the worldly slime, crustaceans, seaweed, and shells was an exquisite marble statue that was the very essence of who "I" was.

**Who is my *I***

I hope by this point in the chapter, you are beginning to wonder what this whole "I", "Me," and true Self means. The next few paragraphs may be conceptually difficult from a psychological and philosophical perspective, but I believe they contain the first principle, the key, that will allow us to find the happiness that resides within.

During the evolution to discover my true Self, my "I" started with a quest to understand the issue of free will, in particular, do I have any? If the answer was no and I was simply a product of my genes and conditioning, why even try? There could be no evolution of consciousness, no happiness; I was simply stuck with my unconscious actions and reactions.

I love the 1999 science fiction thriller, "The Matrix[8]" because it captures my question and struggles perhaps better than any film that has been made. It's a film that delves into a world where reality is not what it seems, raising profound questions about our perception of truth and freedom. One scene that particularly fascinates me is when Morpheus, brilliantly portrayed by Laurence Fishburne, presents Neo, played by Keanu Reeves, with a life-altering choice between a red pill and a blue pill.

In this pivotal moment, Morpheus speaks these powerful words to Neo: "You are a slave, Neo. Like everyone else, you were born into bondage, trapped inside an intangible and imperceptible prison. It is a prison for your mind. This is your last chance. Once you make your choice, there's no turning back. The blue pill will let you continue living in blissful ignorance, accepting the manufactured reality of the Matrix. But if you take the red pill, you will enter Wonderland, where I will show you the profound depths of the rabbit-hole. Remember, all I offer is the truth, nothing more."

In my 2016 book *The Rewired Brain*[5], I highlighted that our lives are not controlled by a computer-generated Matrix, but by the powerful influence of our unconscious mind, often referred to as System 1 with all its out-of-control emotions, feelings, and reactions. Its counterpart is our conscious mind, responsible for System 2 reasoning with its deliberate and controlled mental processes that require attention and effort. My goal in writing the book was to provide a transformative journey of Self-discovery, much like Morpheus does for Neo. I emphasized that exercising free will means making conscious choices about how we want to live. We can remain stuck in the illusions and limitations of the familiar or embrace the path of freedom. The true path to authenticity, love, and liberation lies in taking the metaphorical "red pill." Only by awakening to the depths of our true Self can we navigate the intricacies of life's rabbit-hole. Just as Morpheus offered Neo the truth, I extended the same invitation to you.

However, as I mentioned in the Introduction, during a powerful exchange with an extremely honest woman at a local Barnes & Noble, she pointed out a crucial aspect missing from my book. She acknowledged that it thoroughly explained why our lives can become a mess, unraveling the intricate reasons behind our destructive reactions. However, it failed to offer a solution—a means to overcome these challenges. To her, it was like describing a tumor without providing the tools to treat it. Her words struck a powerful chord within me and set me off on another trail of my evolving journey.

Reflecting on her comments, I realized she was absolutely right. I had to go deeper to better understand the underlying causes of our destructive behaviors and the relationship and interaction between the primary components of my mind. My curiosity and intuition strongly sensed that this was the direction I must move toward to truly empower us to rewrite our narratives, break free from destructive patterns, and find that beautiful happiness we were searching for.

The exploration of the self, particularly the distinction between the "I" and "Me," has been a captivating topic in psychological and philosophical literature, as evidenced by Plato's thought experiment. One prominent, more modern figure who shed light on this concept is William James, often hailed as the "Father of American Psychology." James delved into the depths of psychology and the philosophy of mind, making significant contributions. For James, the "I" symbolized the immediate and intimate experience of self-awareness—the essence of one's being that remains constant throughout life. It encompasses personal choices, initiates actions, and forms decisions. It is the awareness of our own existence intricately intertwined with our stream of consciousness. On the other hand, the "Me" represents the self-concept shaped by social interactions and external influences. It emerges through societal norms, cultural values, and feedback from others. The "Me" involves adopting roles, internalizing expectations, and developing a sense of self based on how others perceive us.

My spiritual evolution took a sharp turn toward a deepening understanding as I dug into the teachings of the great Swiss psychologist Carl Jung, the German-born spiritual teacher Eckhart Tolle, and the Vietnamize Zen master *Thich Nhat Hanh.* Then, I discovered a book called *Awareness*[9], by Anthony de Mello, that heavily impacted my thinking. De Mello, a passionate and radical Jesuit priest and spiritual teacher, brought a fresh perspective on the "I" and "Me" within personal transformation and spiritual awakening. De Mello emphasized the distinction between the true Self, the "I," and the false self associated with the "Me." According to de Mello, the "Me" signifies the conditioned unconscious self—the egoic identity shaped by childhood experiences, societal influences, and external expectations. Conversely, de Mello described the "I" as the authentic Self—the essence of an individual that transcends conditioning, societal constructs, and even time. The "I" is connected to the source of consciousness and represents our true nature.

These understandings deeply resonated with my spiritual evolution, and I found profound solace in them. They provided a clear framework for understanding of the Self in two primary dimensions. Most importantly, this framework provided a mindful awareness approach in which my "I" could act as a powerful antidote to the problems that my "Me" was constantly creating.

What I find truly captivating is the constant presence of the "I" observing the "Me." This phenomenon has always fascinated philosophers, mystics, and psychologists for millennia. This leads us to ask profound questions about our identity. Am I defined by my thoughts, the fleeting mental processes that occur within me? No, thoughts come and go, so they cannot be the essence of who I am. Am I my physical body? As a biologist, I know that millions of cells in our bodies constantly change or renew every minute. Over a decade, very few cells remain the same.

Cells arise and die, but the "I" persist. Therefore, I am not my body. Can I be identified by my name? No, because I can change my name without changing the core of who I am, the "I." What about my roles, career, or beliefs? All of these can change over time, but the "I" remains constant. Does the "I" ever change? Does the Observer within us ever change? Whatever labels we attach to ourselves belong to the "Me," not the "I." The "I" transcends all of these.

Perhaps the most profound realization is that suffering, fear, depression, and even death do not exist within the "I." We can acknowledge that these aspects belong to the "Me," but we cannot attribute them to the essence of the "I" itself. Our "I" remains untouched by suffering, fear, depression, or the inevitable reality of death. It is eternal and transcendent. The depths of our being, our true Self, are beyond the reach of such experiences. This understanding has become a cornerstone of my belief system, reminding me each day of my eternal nature.

I have come to firmly believe that this first principle is the key to unlocking the inherent happiness within us. Therefore, a significant portion of this book will be dedicated to developing this mental and mystical framework. I will delve deeper into the understanding of the "I" and the "Me," exploring their dynamics and how they shape our experiences. Through this exploration, we can uncover the essence of our being and unleash the happiness already within us.

From this point in the book, I will write the "I" or true Self in italics as *I* or *Self*, respectively. I will denote "Me" as *Me* or unconscious self.

# Chapter 2-

# Who Is *Me*?

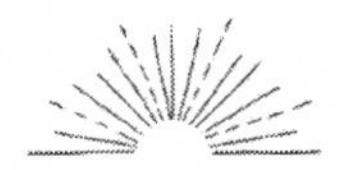

**The "405"**

I have a confession to make. I hate driving in big cities. I know, I know, as a mindfulness practitioner, I shouldn't use words like "hate." So, let me reframe it. The *Me* within me feels fearful and thus strongly dislikes driving in big cities. I believe this fear stems largely from my upbringing in rural North Carolina, where dirt roads and small two-lane highways were the norm. Trips to the big city, such as Winston-Salem, with its population of approximately 100,000 at the time, were rare and filled with excitement and a sense of wonder.

I can vividly recall my first experiences driving in major cities like Atlanta, New York, and Chicago. Even now, the same pit forms in my stomach when I venture out of the rental car area in any large city. However, my most terrifying encounter took place in Los Angeles. It was the day I found myself navigating onto Interstate 405, heading south. Known as "the 405" by city residents, this interstate boasts a staggering fourteen lanes and accommodates approximately 379,000 vehicles each day. That's an immense number of people, goods, and freight moving from one place to another, and it was more than overwhelming for this country boy.

My destination was only a few miles down the Interstate, so my first major mistake was entering the highway and unintentionally merging into the center lanes. Surprisingly, no one seemed willing to allow me to move back into the outer lanes. I sensed a lot of very aggressive and irate versions of *Me* driving those cars. As a result, I could not exit the highway for what felt like an hour, enduring the incessant honking from frustrated drivers who deemed my speed and continuous use of the turn signal as infuriating. Despite having been to some of the most dangerous places in the world while working with nonprofits, I'm not sure I've ever felt as frightened and frustrated as I did that day on that 405.

Now, let's imagine our strongest brain circuits as colossal superhighways, surpassing even the scale of "the 405" multiplied by billions. These mega-superhighways carry millions of nerve signals from one location in the brain to another each day. Interestingly, there also exists a highway construction company known as Neurogenesis, responsible for the capacity of the brain to alter those circuits, known as brain plasticity. This highly efficient company constructs larger superhighways, adding more lanes, new entrance ramps, and removing exit ramps based on the frequency of use for a particular highway. The more a 'highway' or brain circuit is utilized, the more expansive it becomes. Conversely, if a highway lane or exit is utilized less frequently, it receives no additional construction funding and, over time, falls into disrepair and is no longer capable of carrying nerve signals. This very simplified explanation highlights the formation and deconstruction of new nerve circuits (highways) that takes place every minute of your life.

So, if delving into the pages of this book resonates deeply within you, it indicates that you are engaged in a transformative journey beyond mere intellectual exploration. This profound engagement is likely triggering a remarkable process known as epigenetics, where the very DNA of your brain undergoes alterations. Through this process, your brain circuitry or 'highway system' is influenced and reshaped, paving the way for new patterns of thinking, feeling, and being.

**Two Minds in One Brain**

In my previous book, *The Rewired Brain*[5], I discussed how our experiences can shape our neural pathways in ways that can wreak havoc in our lives. This remains a key premise of this book: Our mind is a battlefield of two systems of thought. These systems, often referred to as System 1 and System 2 or the unconscious and conscious minds, tussle for control over our attention, emotions, and actions. In this chapter, I'm going to focus on System 1, the unconscious mind or, as I call it in this book, the *Me*.

The unconscious *Me* is like an invisible puppet master that manipulates us into becoming slaves to our basic survival instincts, all while being swayed by childhood conditioning and external influences like fear-mongering media or certain forms of exclusionary, controlling religion or politics. Meanwhile, the second part of the brain, the conscious mind within the frontal regions of the brain, is a more advanced, uniquely human entity where the *I* resides.

Now, don't be mistaken into thinking these systems are polar opposites - an angel and a devil perched on our shoulders. Each system has a distinct role; both are essential for survival and productivity. But when the scales tip and the *Me* overshadows the *I*, our human experience suffers in profound, painful, and devastating ways.

This *Me* part of our brain, a relic of our evolutionary past, governs primitive, instinctual reactions. It's the heart of the lower (reptilian) and mid (limbic system) brain, controlling survival-focused emotions and reactions like reproduction, protection, control, competition, and pleasure.

One of the most unfair advantages of the unconscious *Me* (as opposed to the conscious *I*) is that it operates lightning-fast, triggering powerful emotions and intuitive reactions to our sensory experiences. Perhaps more insidious, its unconscious nature keeps us largely oblivious to its workings, rendering us unable to reject or change its messages. It's like a steady stream of unconscious signals that we are helpless to stop.

The *Me* is like a vigilant sentry, recalling past threats or harm and alerting us unconsciously through fear or fight-or-flight responses. Its prime directive is survival, with little regard for our happiness. For instance, a child who faced neglect or abandonment from a parent during childhood is highly likely to have an unconscious fear of abandonment and a deep feeling of unworthiness in their adult relationships, all leading to a spiral of heartbreak for this individual and those around him/her.

On a brighter note, the ever-alert *Me* is responsible for spontaneity, aspects of social popularity, and creativity. I call my *Me* my Homer Simpson from the animated sitcom, *The Simpsons*. He will clearly be the life of any party, but you don't want him making important, life-changing decisions when everything is on the line. This part of the brain also seamlessly performs routine tasks like walking and driving.

The unconscious *Me* also plays a crucial role in one of the most basic human instincts—survival of the fittest. This primal need to exert control fuels both positive and many more negative competitive aspects of modern life. Today's "fittest" are often those who amass material possessions, professional achievements, sexual conquests, or elevated social and wealth statuses, and those who disguise their greed as ambition and dominate others in relationships. For instance, my *Me* helped me accomplish a great deal and took great pride in my role as a "world-class scientist." However, as discussed above, this in no way provided a sustainable path to happiness.

**The Monkey Mind**

It is important to point out that the constant dialogue between our unconscious and conscious minds is made possible by an intricate network of neural circuits, 'wires', or 'highway lanes', if we use the 405 analogy at the beginning of this chapter. Our thoughts, responses, reactions, and even our personalities are shaped through these interactions. Intriguingly and highly relevant to our discussion, these circuits are not fixed; they can be reshaped or rewired by our experiences and our fresh thoughts and ideas. This malleability of our brain's circuitry is known as neuroplasticity, a groundbreaking concept in neuroscience. A cornerstone principle here is that the more intense an experience or routine a habit is, the stronger its associated brain circuit. And as you exercise this circuit more, it grows stronger and larger. And this is how addictions are formed, whether they be emotional or otherwise. On the flip side, circuits that aren't used and the behaviors and emotions they trigger tend to weaken.

With its ceaseless flood of unconscious signals, the unconscious *Me* is a potent entity that seems to have all the advantages. As its functions can't be turned off, it typically wins the tug of war against reasoned and conscious thoughts.

I can't even begin to count how many times I've heard this one: "Oh, Dr. Ski, I could never meditate. I can't even sit still for 30 seconds, let alone clear my mind." This is a common refrain, one that I empathize with because I've been there. It took me 3 months of meditation practices before I could sit on a meditation cushion for more than 5 minutes.

This, my friends, is the classic hallmark of what's known in the world of mindfulness as the "Monkey Mind." Originating from Buddhist teachings, the term "Monkey Mind" paints a pretty vivid picture, doesn't it? Just like a monkey rapidly vaults from branch to branch in a tree, our minds skip from thought to thought in a restless, agitated manner. Our minds, left on their own, just go crazy.

This restless, unsettled state of mind is filled with ceaseless chatter, bouncing aimlessly and without control. It is clearly the source of anxiety, worry, and distraction. The Monkey Mind can manifest itself in several ways: racing thoughts, constant self-doubt, the inability to stay focused, or a ceaseless internal monologue. We spend so much of our mental energy ruminating about the past or worrying about the future, which completely blocks our ability to sense the present moment.

If you are currently not a seasoned meditator, or even if you are, I want you to sit still for 5 minutes and watch what is happening in your head. What a mess! This, my friends, is your Monkey Mind, your unconscious *Me* running the show, robbing you of any chance of joy and tranquility.

This 'Sh#! Show' is happening every second of every day of our lives. This gives us some idea of what we are up against. Frankly, I find it amazing that we don't all go mad.

I remember when I became curious about mindfulness, and I went to a practitioner and asked them who was the local expert who could teach me to meditate. I had only a few weeks to become enlightened, and I needed to be taught by the best. Boy, was I naïve! This reminds me of the young graduate student who walked into my office one day and said, "Teach me biochemistry." I just smiled at the poor lad and asked, "Do you have a lifetime to learn?"

Ideally, our conscious minds, in theory, should be able to reign in the unconscious *Me*, acting with some executive control. However, achieving any influence requires effort and discipline, employing mindfulness and meditation tools such as those found in the CAST Process practices at the end of this book. Through these practices, individuals learn to calm their minds, observe their thoughts without attaching to them, and bring their attention back to the present moment. This, in turn, eases anxiety, improves focus, and allows the happiness within our *I* to come to the surface.

**We Have Free Will until We Don't**

I frequently share this nugget of wisdom, "The stories we tell ourselves shape our realities, so be very mindful of the narratives you feed yourself." We'll dive deeper into this concept in Chapter 5, but let's briefly discuss it as we wrap up this chapter.

Now, whenever I mention that I spent a year deep diving into the concept of free will and its existence, people typically respond, "In your opinion, do we have it (free will) or not?" My response? "Well, it depends." Every time we tell a story or behave in a way that echoes the less appealing aspects of our unconscious *Me*, we essentially trigger genetic (actually epigenetic) changes in our brain's DNA. This, in turn, activates genes (Neurogenesis Company) that produce proteins (Neurogenesis work crews) that 'wire' and 'strengthen' certain nerve circuits, making it more likely that we will make the same choice again. In other words, each consistent choice or action reinforces the likelihood of us reacting in similar ways in the future.

Remember the analogy of the "405" freeway I started this chapter with? I asked you to picture our brain's strongest nerve pathways as enormous superhighways, dwarfing even "the 405." This colossal nerve circuitry transports millions of nerve signals across our brain regions each day. As discussed above, an in-brain construction crew is proficient at expanding highways, adding more lanes, introducing new entry points, and removing exit ramps—all based on how frequently a particular nerve superhighway circuit is used. The more it is utilized, the larger it grows.

So now here is my answer to the free will question. "Yes, I believe we initially can make undetermined responses or reactions to different situations." One of the "self-forming" choices could be to downplay the situation's significance and decide not to react, but even that is a form of response. Importantly, we also may change our choice if the initial one continues to bring hardships and havoc to our lives or others. In doing this, we maintain our capacity to make free choices.

However, over time, consistent responses become permeant due to their ability to accumulate the epigenetic changes in our brain DNA, leading to subsequent, at a certain point, irreversible changes to our brain circuitry. With each reliable response to a type of situation, we become more prone to exhibit that same deterministic, unconscious reaction in the future.

Ultimately, consistent responses and reactions transform brain architecture, leading to deterministic, predictive unconscious reactions. At this point, we have largely lost our "ability to choose otherwise" or, said another way, our free will. Essentially, we have free will until our decisions construct such vast highways in our brains that we don't. The consistency of our choices and our stories forge our character.

To specifically illustrate this, I often caution folks about the dangers of viewing themselves as victims. Embracing victimhood is treacherous because it often initially gives something back to the victim. People sympathize with you, shower you with attention, perform kind acts—all of which only serve to reinforce the brain circuits that reinforce your victimhood narrative. But heed my warning—take one step too far down this path, and victimhood will become your only option.

The above processes critically influence our responses, reactions, and, ultimately, our character. Chapters 4, 5, and 6 will delve into specific areas where we may have unknowingly cultivated a negative and painful unconscious *Me*, using the processes described here. Each of these areas can cause misery in our lives and obstruct any possibility of finding peace and happiness.

# Chapter 3 -

# Finding the *I* within My *Me* Storm

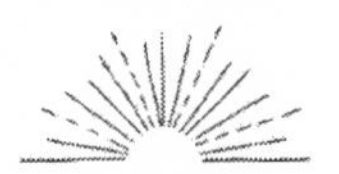

### A Hurricane

I have always been fascinated by the forces of nature, and hurricanes, in particular, have held a peculiar allure for me. It may sound strange, but I had always had a desire to experience the raw power of a hurricane firsthand. A few years ago, I was granted that very opportunity. My sailboat was located at the mouth of Pimlico Sound in the Outer Banks of North Carolina, an area known for its frequent encounters with these tempestuous storms. These barrier islands bear the brunt of a hurricane's force approximately once every two years.

In preparation for the impending storm, I needed to relocate my sailboat slightly inland, anchoring it in a river to ensure its safety amidst the looming winds and storm surge. My neighbors, seasoned inhabitants of the Outer Banks, assured me that this was the only way to safeguard my boat from imminent destruction. As the hurricane drew near, we all sought refuge in a fortified boathouse, anxiously monitoring our phones for updates on the latest storm's location.

The increasing intensity of the storm caught me off guard. I was astounded as the counterclockwise winds gradually approached from the south. Over the next few hours, the winds grew in ferocity, compelling us to venture out ever so briefly to check on the state of our boats. At its peak, the wind speed surpassed 90 mph, and I can still vividly recall the haunting sound resembling a freight train whistle piercing through the air. Equally awe-inspiring was the sight of the water surging into the river, effortlessly lifting my 6-ton boat as if it were a mere play toy.

Then, suddenly, the chaos ceased. The seasoned locals assured me that the eyewall of the hurricane was upon us, and a period of eerie tranquility was imminent. I rushed outside to witness this phenomenon and was astounded as I gazed upward and was greeted by not black clouds but a serene moon and stars. At that moment, everything was so still, disconcertingly calm. How could such serenity coexist amidst the chaos of winds, water, and devastation? This paradox continues to amaze me to this day.

Allow your imagination to transport you to a day without pressure and anxiety. Picture yourself strolling through nature or enjoying a day at the beach, devoid of obligations and commitments. During such moments, your inner landscape becomes unburdened. There is no external force pushing or oppressing you. Anxiety, duties, roles, and stress dissipate. Nothing attempts to mold you into something or someone you are not. In this space in the center of your being, you experience peace.

However, as discussed in the last chapter, this is not the typical state of our lives. Normally, we find ourselves caught in a web of triumph and failure, panic and exaltation, pain and relief. Living life combined with our powerful, unrelenting unconscious minds of our *Me* can feel like a category 5 hurricane is constantly upon us, with the darkened sky and the roaring power relentlessly advancing. It metaphorically lifts roofs, topples telephone poles and streetlights, and destroys homes and cars. Emotional winds reaching 150 mph and a 20-foot anxiety storm surge disrupt and destroy everything in their path.

Yet, in the center, in the eye of the storm, an inexplicable calm exists. Amidst the metaphysical *I* in the hurricane of life, not a breath of wind stirs. The sky is clear, and a protective wall of clouds surrounds this pocket of tranquility. I believe this can represent a powerful analogy for the human condition. The hurricane symbolizes our unconscious turbulent feelings giving rise to unending, incessantly looping thoughts and fears, while the eye, the *I* of the storm, represents the serene refuge that we long for. This is where our joy and peace reside.

The rest of this book will be devoted to how we can return to the center, to the eye, to the *I*, to rejuvenate ourselves, and find our innate happiness. Life and our minds pull us in a thousand different directions, disorganizing and distracting us, filling us with fear and anxiety amidst our seemingly ceaseless obligations. In this age of constant stimuli, social media, politics, and news cycles, each designed to frighten us, we very rapidly lose contact with our center, our *I*.

In this overstimulated place, our *Me* insists on such urgency and demands all of our attention. Driven by this force, we frantically rush about, and instead of reducing our tasks, they just seem to multiply. By its very nature, life is messy and unruly, but our unconscious *Me* makes it unbearable. That is precisely why we must learn how to return to the center, our *I,* to find our *Self* once more. In that center, in the stillness of the present moment, a perpetual holiday awaits.

**A Holiday at the Sea**

This idea of an uninterrupted joyful holiday reminds me of a quote from *The Weight of Glory*[10] by CS Lewis "We are half-hearted creatures, fooling about with drink and sex and ambition when infinite joy is offered us, like an ignorant child who wants to go on making mud pies in a slum because he cannot imagine what is meant by the offer of a holiday at the sea. We are far too easily pleased."

Our *Me* plays a significant role in our sense of half-heartedness. Our deeply ingrained patterns, fears, attachments, and conditioning reside within the depths of the unconscious, shaping our very perception of reality. We find ourselves unable to imagine anything different, trapped within the confines of what we know. Our unconscious *Me* consistently pushes us toward the familiar, even if it brings us unhappiness. It discourages us from venturing outside our comfort zones and embarking on a transformative journey, no matter how dissatisfied we may be with our current lives. It taunts us with the notion that it is better to stick with the known devil than to risk encountering an unknown one. This very resistance keeps us trapped in the slums, content with making mud pies while a magnificent holiday at the sea awaits us.

Solving this greatest of all problems requires us to transcend the plane on which the problem is created. Attempting to unravel a problem from within its grasp only intensifies the confusion and despair, leaving us stuck and stagnant. To overcome our half-heartedness, we must acknowledge the influence of our unconscious mind and then step outside its grip. We must recognize how our fears, conditioning, and attachments shape our perceptions and choices. This awareness becomes the catalyst for challenging and surpassing the limitations that hold us back.

Awareness, then disidentification, becomes our keys to freedom. We learn to detach ourselves from the difficulties that entangle us, allowing them to dissipate as we retreat to the center, the essence of our being and the *I*. In the sanctuary of the *I*, we find solace and strength. It becomes our shield from the commotion of daily life and the chaos our *Me* creates from it, rendering them distant and impotent.

**The Observer**

In the Introduction, I described an unexpected yet crucial aspect of my mindfulness journey – the silent, eternal companion known as the Observer, or the "witness consciousness" found in Eastern spirituality. This entity, intrinsic to my *I,* initially bore striking resemblances to my Western concept of "consciousness," but I soon found that there were profound differences that set them apart.

Indeed, the Western "conscious" and the Eastern "Observer" play fundamental roles in self-awareness, acting as internal mirrors reflecting our life experiences. However, their nature also diverges significantly. Living with a conscious throughout my life, I recognized its propensity to observe activities, but it had an embedded moral compass. While it guided me through a maze of ethical dilemmas, separating right from wrong, my *Me* internalized the judgments from my conscious.

Importantly, this internalization came at a significant emotional cost. I have spent a large part of my life believing I was a "bad" person due to my mistakes. Given our human predisposition to err and inadvertently cause harm, my conscious made me feel that I was a callous, uncaring man at my core. This self-perception was a primary driver of much of my anxiety and depression. Despite my earnest efforts to be a good man, I found myself making mistakes and hurting others, and this naturally produced overwhelming guilt and self-reproach.

In stark contrast, the Observer was a compassionate witness adopting a non-judgmental stance, merely seeing, without attaching judgments or forming attachments to my actions. It accompanied me, empathetically observing my struggles, even when I faltered, as we all inevitably do. Instead of chastising me for my indiscretions, it seemed to convey a comforting message: "It's okay; it's hard to be human." Through this awareness and in the absence of judgment, we can evolve, and our lives will improve. We learn important lessons through each mistake and heartache; we begin to comprehend and gain confidence that life, despite its struggles, is guiding us to where we need to be.

I now realize that the Observer was (is) a vital part of my *I* and that it had always been in me. The Observer possessed a gentle awareness. The Observer approached every thought that passed through my mind, every word that came out of my mouth, every action I took, and every mistake I made, with a sympathetic, impartial gaze. It saw no dichotomies of good or bad, right or wrong. It simply bore witness to what was devoid of labels and judgments. In its company, I began to appreciate reality's unadorned, naked essence from a tolerant, loving, forgiving perspective.

Oh, I can feel my religious friends judging me right now as they read these words. I would remind that before we Christians' judge, examining Jesus' non-judgmental teachings on full display throughout the gospels is critical. These stories that I have been taught from childhood echo within me, and they powerfully resonate with the characteristics of the Observer within me.

Why? Take, for instance, the tale of the woman accused of adultery in John 8:1-11. Jesus found himself in a crowd quick to cast stones—both literally and metaphorically—at this woman. Yet, in the face of this spectacle of judgment, he responded with unexpected grace and mercy with his words, "He that is without sin among you, let him first cast a stone at her." When no stones were thrown, and the crowd dissolved, Jesus turned to the woman and told her that he also did not condemn her life, but perhaps it would be better if she took a better path. There was not judgment, but the steering by her increased awareness.

Similarly, in the story of the Prodigal Son from Luke 15:11-32, Jesus described a father who embodied the very essence of non-judgment. Despite the younger son's reckless abandonment and squandering of his inheritance in a world of 'sin', the father welcomed his return without a shred of condemnation. This tale of unadulterated love and acceptance is untainted by the bitter tang of judgment.

Jesus's interactions were with those deemed by society as sinners; in every instance, he demonstrated his non-judgmental, compassionate nature. Instead of shunning these individuals, he spent time with them, showing them love and understanding that overshadowed societal judgments and labels. These are all like lanterns to me, illuminating the path of non-judgment, love, and understanding.

It saddens me as I struggle to comprehend the transformation within much of modern-day Christianity, which seems to have increasingly centered itself around judgment and condemnation. How and why did such a profound shift occur? As Forrest Gump would eloquently put it, "that's all I have to say about that." This topic is indeed a vast ocean unto itself, deserving of its own separate exploration—perhaps the subject of another book.

As I have journeyed further into the expansive landscape of spirituality, I'm continually intrigued by overlaps and alignments between various religious traditions and philosophies. One connection that's particularly sparked my curiosity is between the mysterious and mystical Holy Spirit of the Bible and the Observer in Eastern spirituality.

In Christian teachings, the Holy Spirit, imparted following Jesus's death, serves as a comforting presence, a guiding hand, and a wellspring of wisdom. Sounds familiar, doesn't it? In my view, what we call this ever-present aspect of our consciousness - whether we call this entity the Observer or the Holy Spirit doesn't matter. What's significant is recognizing this part of the *I* is in us. This inner, compassionate Observer can be found at the center of the hurricane of our unconscious *Me*, providing awareness, clarity, understanding, and guidance.

It maintains a pure and peaceful stance, overseeing our thoughts and actions without judgment, thereby fostering compassion, kindness, and balance. While remaining an untouched presence within life's storms, it, through awareness, allows us to navigate through the blinding fog of our emotions and difficult experiences, eventually leading us to the illusive happiness that is present within us all.

**Be Still and Know**

As I deepened my relationship with the Observer, primarily through meditations and getting back into nature, I discovered its remarkable ability to sit or walk with me in stillness in the present moment. It is unburdened by past regrets or future anxieties; instead, it is fully immersed in the 'here and now'. These practices of 'present-moment awareness' unshackled me from the chains of time, allowing me to savor the sweet nectar of the present in almost any situation.

With a reassuring constancy, the Observer was always there— a beacon of continuity in the ever-changing landscape of my thoughts, fears, emotions, and sensations. Amidst the ebb and flow of our existence, of our unconscious *Me*, it stands as the unchanging aspect of my consciousness, my *I*, providing a timeless whisper amidst the chaotic shouts of everyday life.

Sometimes, my kids think I've gone off the deep end—and perhaps I have, but I believe in a beautifully unconventional way of life. Once I crossed the threshold of 60 years of age, I started adorning myself with tattoos—not just for aesthetics, but as unique reminders for my true *Self* of what truly mattered. Want to take a wild guess at what my first tattoo was? It featured the Alpha and Omega symbols, the first and the last, the beginning and the end, encapsulated by the profoundly simple yet powerful words: "Be Still and Know."

This tattoo is a constant reminder, guiding me back into the present moment and awareness. It nudges me to anchor myself with the Observer in the 'now', to be still amidst the whirlwind of life's challenges and uncertainties. The Alpha and Omega symbolize the continuity of existence, reminding me that within the present moment and across the vast expanse of eternity, all I need to do is to be still. When I allow myself to settle into this stillness, I find that I am bestowed with all the knowledge necessary for life's journey, just in time, for each unfolding moment.

**What's Next?**

So far, much of the content of this book has revolved around the confusion, complexity, and challenges our human condition. However, as the woman in the Barnes and Nobel bookstore rightly nudged, or perhaps shoved, it's high time that we pivot our attention to healing, to mending the parts of us that have been bruised and battered, and ultimately, to unveiling a path towards peace and happiness.

# Step 2 -

# Deepening <u>A</u>wareness

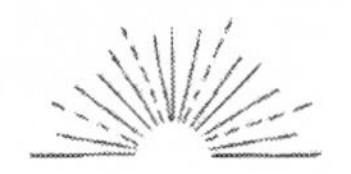

As we have already discovered from the previous chapters, most of us traverse through life unconscious of our actions. Socrates once voiced that "an unexamined life is not worth living", a sentiment I deeply resonate with. We unknowingly find ourselves within the cramped confines of a small prison cell constructed by our unconscious minds, painful conditioning, and deceptive narratives. Simultaneously, our authentic *Self*, our *I,* stands adjacent to these self-imposed cells, key in hand, yearning to liberate us. The key to waking up from our bad dream will be *deepening* ***A****wareness*.

The chapters within Step 2 of the CAST Process were written to illuminate the specific mechanisms and blueprints that our unconscious minds employ to maintain our imprisoning walls. By increasing awareness of the critical areas where pain and deception are birthed, we will begin to comprehend that freedom lies not merely in self-discovery but, more importantly, in identifying and dismantling untruths. This is necessary because these falsehoods are the major factor that leads to our fear, anxiety, and ceaseless river of negative thinking.

This segment of the book is engineered to assist you in unmasking the occupants of your *Me*. The unveiling can be both harrowing and painful. We are often so ensnared in the illusion of freedom, but truthfully, we are shackled. An enormous amount of awareness will be required to grasp that this entity *we perceive as our true self* is a construct, a mosaic of past experiences, conditioning, and programming. It is a powerful mind-made self that effectively obstructs the joy and peace nestled within us.

While this will likely be the most difficult part of the book for most of us, I also want to inspire hope. Any pain and discomfort you may feel as you delve into observing details of your past, your conditioning, and the self you've—we've all—fabricated is necessary. I assure you that the awareness gained here will soon be transformed into a graceful dance partner, guiding you towards liberation, unimaginable growth, and authentic happiness.

# Chapter 4 -

# Fear and Childhood Trauma

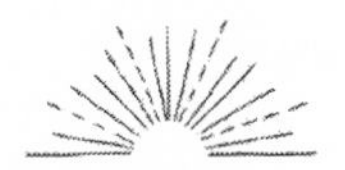

## 'Shadow' Work

As you already know, I am profoundly committed to meditation. Without it, I truly believe there are times that I would descend into madness. At least a couple of times a day, you'll find me meditating, typically using a highly popular meditation app, "Insight Timer." According to my app, I've had 2,337 sessions over the past three years, which translates to a frequency of just over two times per day. That's a cumulative 595 hours or approximately 25 full days of non-stop meditation. And that's just on my Insight Timer app. This is why I am so passionate about the transformative power of the CAST Process and meditation/ mindfulness practices.

Almost every day, I'll put in my earbuds and embark on a one-mile walk across the University of Arizona campus to my favorite coffee shop, accompanied by a guided meditation. A couple of years ago, I was intrigued by the concept of inner child or 'shadow' work advocated by practitioners like Catherine Liggett[11]. So, I decided to try one of her meditations. I thought in jest, how much trauma could there be from my hardworking but otherwise 'very happy' childhood? I simply listened to understand what everyone else was talking about.

On this particular day, I had just received the disheartening news that one of my NIH grants would not be funded. The news hit me hard, stirring up feelings of deep inadequacy. I felt immense shame and disgrace. Despite my rational understanding that approximately 85% of all NIH grants are not funded the first time around, these feelings persisted. Where were these coming from?

As I began my walk, listening to Catherine's soothing, melodic guidance, she instructed me to breathe with my body and notice how that felt. She asked me to pay attention to any areas of tension or aliveness within my body, to invite in whatever emotions were present, and to let them expand and intensify. Again, on this particular day, the feelings of shame and unworthiness reemerged, and my all-too-familiar 'impostor syndrome' was taking over.

Catherine then guided me to hold on to this "feeling signature" in my heart and to call upon an earlier memory in my life when I had experienced the same or similar feelings. And that's when I found him, a small boy of eight or nine, lying in a tiny corner of a room, his gaze fixed on a spot where the floor met the wall. He quietly sobbed, whispering, "Why won't they play with me?" "Why am I always the last one picked in basketball?" "I'm so ugly with my Coke bottle glasses." "Everyone else can read but me. I'm just a dumb, ugly duckling everyone picks on and makes fun of." "I have no one to play with." "What's wrong with me?" "Nobody loves me." "I'm just a great big loser!"

I was stunned by what I witnessed and found myself weeping uncontrollably beneath a grand tree in the heart of our campus. I thought to myself, surely these feelings will diminish if I simply let them be—isn't that what all my spiritual teachers tell me? Yet these emotions only amplified as the child's feelings connected with mine. Despite my discomfort, I continued what felt like a bad drug trip, only without drugs. I consciously worked to further release and soften my resistance. I then began to sense that I was watching my adult self viewing a child version of me.

But how could that be? I yearned to see the child's eyes. I've always had big, blue eyes, which were always hidden behind thick glasses that could only partially correct my vision. I so wanted the child to remove his glasses and look at me, desperately needing to confirm my suspicion. Sensing my desire, the child turned his head, removed his glasses, and I was able to recognize my child self.

We locked eyes, and a wave of intense sadness and shame washed over me. My child self suffered from uncorrectable vision, preventing him from playing sports like the other kids. He was constantly picked on, unable to retaliate. Severe dyslexia in rural North Carolina, where no one even knew what dyslexia was, completely prevented him from learning to read. As a result, he was stuck in beginner books, color-coded for different reading levels. He never advanced beyond the beginner aquamarine level and was nicknamed "dummy", or "dumb-ass", later on when the kids became crueler. As I mentioned in the Introduction, this little boy, with his dyslexia, would eventually end up in the white building designated for the so-called "unfortunates."

As my adult self, I looked into the eyes of my child self, offering him the love and validation I knew he'd never experienced before. I sensed he desperately needed it. Silently, I spoke to him, "I know you feel like nobody loves you and so ashamed. I see that all this hurts so bad. I see you're alone all the time. I see that you blame yourself for all of this. I see your sadness, and I know you are scared to death."

Once I felt like I had calmed and soothed him, I looked at him tenderly, reassuring him it was okay to feel this way. "It's okay, little buddy. You've already been through so much. Any child who went through what you did would feel the same. There's nothing wrong with you feeling this way."

I revealed to the child that I was his future self and was here to support him. "It's going to be okay. You'll show them all one day. I promise!" Following Catherine's advice, I offered, "I'm here to give you what you need. So, tell me, what do you need right now?"

The child looked back at me and simply said, "I want to be loved. I want to be accepted and feel acceptable." I told him that he was, and he was so precious, and he had no idea of the gifts he would one day see. He would be a college athlete, a great scientist, and he would write books that would help people all around the world. He seemed to doubt what I was saying, but I assured him all this was the truth. By the end, I seemed to have provided him with exactly what he needed in a way he could understand.

I then asked, "Is there anything else I can do for you?" Sensing his need for physical comfort, I felt him nod as he ran across the room as fast as he could to hug me. As I held him close, I reassured him, "You will never be alone again. I will always be here with you. I will support you no matter what. While my adult consciousness may shift away from you from time to time, you will always live in my heart with me."

After a couple more hours under that tree, I gathered myself and returned to my office. As I walked back, I kept thinking, "If he was in there, were there other versions of me at different ages and times?" As I was to discover with the help of my compassionate counselor, Maureen, the answer was a resounding "Yes!"

I have spent significant time meeting and consoling these beautiful, hurting, and vulnerable younger versions of me, each a snapshot of trauma at a different time and place in my life. I also realize that my journey is far from over. This is our first chapter in Step 2 "Deepening Awareness," and I suspect I may not be the only one who desperately needs to connect with their inner child.

### The Power of Fear

To better understand what could have created that frightened and shame-filled little child in me and childhood trauma in general, we must appreciate the capacity of fear to shape and condition us. Buried within our subconscious survival instincts, fear acts as a potent force, shaping our deepest, most painful emotions and behaviors. As I have discussed above, the brain circuitry for fear is found within the primitive regions of our brain, facilitating human survival. It helped our forebears dodge threats or resort to violence for self-protection, stimulating fight-or-flight responses. Apart from its physical manifestations, fear is marked by terror, dread, and anxiety, forever forecasting doom. While fear can arise from real, immediate dangers, it often stems from challenging, neglectful, or abusive past experiences in our modern context. These experiences condition us subconsciously to anticipate similar threats ahead, forming powerful emotions tied to the original fear-inducing events.

Fear wields its disruptive power through two elusive aspects. First, we often lack clear recollections of the incidents that incited fear; yet, we sense their unconscious effects in our daily lives. In some cases, the events were so traumatic that they have been suppressed or trivialized. I recently talked with a friend who insisted that she enjoyed a 'great childhood'. When pressed, she revealed that her father would not allow her and her siblings to talk at the dinner table, reacting with a shout of "shut up!" if they did. She also recounted instances of her father's physical and emotional abuse towards her mother, often escalating to the point where he would threaten her mother with a gun. Her older sister would then secretly dial 911 to alert the police. In response to my concern about this unhealthy childhood environment, she said that she simply chose to focus on the less painful, more pleasant memories.

The second deceptive aspect of fear, which stems from its origin in our primitive brain, is that it lacks the capability for critical assessment. As I pointed out above, for those with a history of childhood trauma or neglect, these early experiences can give rise to intense unconscious fears and emotions that persist in our adult lives. My younger self desperately sought love, acceptance, and a sense of worth. That fear was continually providing a clear but highly inaccurate message to my adult self. "Ski, if you accomplish enough, you will eventually feel worthy and be acceptable." The adult me tried to fulfill this deep-seated drive for nearly four decades. Although my achievements built an incredibly impressive résumé by any standard, it couldn't fill the gaping void of unworthiness within me. I had bet everything on accolades and accomplishments. The realization that none of these could provide happiness only deepened my despair, leading to a profound depression and relational failures.

It was only after that critical afternoon when my adult me met a much younger me under a grand tree on our campus that I understood the source of my unworthiness. After that sacred encounter, I realized I could have won a Nobel Prize, and I would have still felt unacceptable. As long as that beautiful little child in me did not feel love and acceptance, there could be no joy in the adult me.

Our early traumas and fears have a great capacity to set off a cascade of mental health issues in adulthood, including depression, anxiety, and post-traumatic stress disorder (PTSD), among others. Additionally, they can trigger intense emotional responses and profoundly impact our romantic relationships, often surfacing as co-dependency tendencies, difficulty setting boundaries, fear of abandonment, and self-sabotage.

As I pen this chapter, I'm taken aback by the number of emotional traps I seem naturally inclined towards. I now recognize that I still, from time to time, deal with feelings of unworthiness and instinctively sway towards co-dependency and excessive people-pleasing. However, my dear friends, I've now gained the ability and awareness to identify these patterns. This recognition is the gateway to a deeper understanding and eventual healing. It's quite common to feel overwhelmed during the type of self-analysis we are doing in this book due to the hyper-focus on our perceived imperfections. Yet, it's crucial that as we navigate through the CAST Process, we maintain a positive attitude and stay focused on our ultimate goal. We've all had past experiences that have shaped our maladaptive beliefs and behaviors. Awareness of our conditioning and the emotional direction in which it moves us is our most important weapon and the key to our enhanced understanding, emotional stability, and happiness.

However, a word of caution is important at this point in the book. A close friend recently confided, " 'shadow' work is not for cowards. If your childhood was as traumatic as mine, you're about to encounter your worst nightmares again as an adult." I completely agree with her. Diving into inner child work and uncovering the fears, traumas, and the people involved in these events takes extraordinary courage and is one of the most difficult things I have ever done. I strongly recommend that this be done under the guidance of a skilled therapist or counselor. This is not a path to tread lightly or alone, but with the right support, it is a path that can lead to self-discovery, healing, and freedom.

**Moving Beyond Our Conditioning**

David Hawkins, a psychiatrist, spiritual teacher, and author, has influenced my perspectives on emotions, particularly through his book *Letting Go: The Pathway of Surrender*[12]. He developed a 'map of consciousness', which describes emotions on an energy spectrum, proposing that emotions like shame and guilt are low-frequency while emotions like love and joy are high-frequency. He said higher frequency emotions are associated with greater spiritual and personal growth.

Hawkins advocated a process of releasing or letting go of emotions as a method of ascending the scale towards more positive emotions. This approach involved objectively observing one's emotions, acknowledging their presence, and then letting them naturally dissipate, aligning with the CAST Process's core principles.

While, as a scientist, I have difficulty with his concepts of energy and how he measured it in individuals, his emotional framework makes a great deal of sense to me. In *Letting Go*[12], Hawkins constructed a scale for different levels of consciousness, ranging from one to 1000, with complete enlightenment at the top, represented by spiritual avatars such as Jesus, Buddha, and Krishna. At the very bottom of the scale is shame, given the numerical value of 20. He suggested that the level of courage, at 200, marks the critical shift from negative to positive consciousness levels. Consciousness levels below courage are destructive to the individual and those around them, while levels above courage strengthen both the individual and others.

For example, peace, joy, and acceptance are high on the scale while apathy, guilt, and shame fall below courage. Why is shame so low? Hawkins states shame is typified by humiliation, as if "hanging your head in shame." It often results in banishment or imprisonment, and it is destructive to health and leads to cruelty towards oneself and others. Individuals who have experienced significant childhood trauma often suffer from shameful feelings as adults.

I find it fascinating and more than coincidental that courage is the balance point between the negative and positive. I believe it sits here because courage is the primary antidote to fear. By letting go of negative feelings produced by fear, we can progressively ascend the scale toward courage and beyond. As we move higher, achieving success is more effortless, and it begins to feel natural. We also innately begin to seek out like-minded people. Individuals at higher levels of consciousness seem to radiate life energy, and it is instantly recognized. They often attract animals, have green thumbs, and seem to elevate all of those around them.

For me, I seemed to have found courage, or courage has found me, several times in my life, and these have been typically associated with very difficult backdrops. In the Introduction, I described my most recent one after my violent encounter with a horse that nearly killed me and fractured my pelvis in half. I was devastated physically and emotionally, so I would go outside each morning at 5:30 a.m. in my wheelchair. With each sunrise, I would sit in stillness in a meditative space, presenting my brokenness to the power of awareness and surrender. Rather than running from discomfort, I confronted it head-on, embracing it within my awareness and letting go of any control regarding my future. As the weeks unfolded, the pain lessened and was replaced by newfound strength and trust.

While we haven't quite reached Step 3, the "Art of Surrender," I'd like to highlight a vital element of courage. This is our ability to surrender our relentless desire for control. This truth struck me more profoundly than ever on my first journey to Sudan, Africa. It was 2009, and I had been asked to join the Board of Directors of a non-profit organization working in Sudan. I was to accompany our relief team to our staging compound just south of Darfur. Darfur was the epicenter of a recent historical genocide that led to approximately 500,00 people killed and another 3 million displaced. I knew before I left that we would fly almost 8 hours through a no-fly zone where we could be shot out of the air, carrying several tons of supplies in an old windowless Russian cargo plane known as an Antonov. We then would land on an 800-meter dirt runway in a region just miles from where northern Sudanese government-armed tribesman, known as the Janjaweed, were murdering and raping tens of thousands of darker-skinned, unarmed 'African' farmers.

As I sat alone in Philadelphia International Airport preparing to board my initial flight to Nairobi, Kenya, I was frightened to the point of weeping as I called each of my children and told them how much I loved them and goodbye. They had no idea what their crazy daddy was about to do, and I was not about to tell them. After the calls, I sensed that this was what I was being called to do, and I said aloud, "I surrender my fear to You." Upon Surrendering (Step 3 in the CAST Process), the fear left me. From that point on, it was as if I was having an out-of-body experience, and I was watching this man (who resembled me) and his friends get medical supplies and food to Darfur for these beautiful, devastated people.

In this context, it's important to note that my fears were not misplaced or exaggerated. My apprehensions about the journey ahead were valid, and the profound sadness I felt at the thought of potentially never seeing my children again was absolutely justified. I share this experience to illustrate how the potent combination of courage, followed by surrender, can empower us to forge ahead through life's most frightening experiences. Whether we're stepping into an incredibly dangerous situation, like my time in Darfur, or facing the haunting nightmares of our childhood traumas, this holds true. Both circumstances can provoke intense fear.

So, how do we move beyond our fears to higher levels of consciousness? I believe this journey involves all steps of the CAST Process. As we become more **C**onscious, we gain the capacity to deepen our **A**wareness of negative emotions and resulting reactions that were driven by some form of fear (often from our inner child). When we sense fear through the lens of awareness, we can be courageous and consciously **S**urrender that fear to a higher power (such as God or the Universe). In my experience, this dramatically increases our confidence and **T**rust (Step 4). This Process, in turn, creates a positive chain reaction; we now have the capacity to exhibit more courage that enables us to move up the emotional scale even further, eventually experiencing predominantly the freedom and happiness that naturally reside in our higher levels of consciousness.

**Jessie's Freedom**

One of the highlights of each day is returning home from work to meet my dog, Jessie, who waits for me by the door. Jessie has taught me more about mindfulness than all my spiritual teachers combined. She is so happy, has no fear, and is filled with unconditional love. Whenever I walk in the door, she takes my hand gently into her mouth, leads me to her leash, and we are off to the golf course near our home for our magical evening walk. After we get to a fairway on the golf course, I say, "Jessie, stay." She stops and looks up at me. Then I unhook her leash and say, "Go!" At that point, young Jessie takes off running at top speed with absolute exuberance, darting around back and forth and then toward me, daring me to catch her, which, of course, would be absolutely impossible.

As I watch her so filled with freedom, joy, and excitement, I wonder how this daily activity could produce so much pleasure for her day after day. It occurs to me that perhaps Jesse has forgotten that she has ever run before, and each evening, it is as if she were running for the first time. An alternative explanation, which I really believe, is that Jessie is so mindful that her happiness can never be diminished by past or current fear, and thus life never loses its splendor. If anything, her joy just becomes more jubilant each day. This thought of Jessie as a Zen Master makes me giggle and wonder how she hangs out with someone as unconscious as me day after day. *I am so grateful that she does!*

# Chapter 5 -

# A Mind-Made Prison

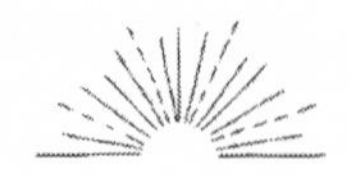

### The Dog I Feed the Most

Remember back in Chapter 1, I spoke about a thought experiment that Plato had put forth more than 2000 years ago comparing us, our true *Self,* our *I,* to a great work that had been at the bottom of the sea, hidden by the accumulation of a lifetime of slime, crustaceans, seaweed, and shells to the point that we had now become a grotesque, hardened monster. However, underneath, a stunning masterpiece still resides, chiseled in beautiful marble by an exceptionally skilled sculptor. Similarly, beneath the surface, we remain unseen, unexperienced, unable to truly experience.

As long as this sacred part of us lies forgotten, buried under layers and layers of debris, we are not free. Not only do others see the imposter we've become, but as we become more aware, we sense the tiny prison cells with only a minuscule window barely providing any light or perspective on the real world. Sadly, these are the prisons that we have built for ourselves. Breaking out of these cells and leading an all-out rebellion while taking as many people as possible requires us to wake up.

As I said earlier, I believe in our modern world, the only way we can discover who we truly are is to discover who we are not. To discover who we are not, we must peel away the coatings that our beliefs, society, conditioning, habits, fears, and self-talk have programmed us to be. These layers of slime must be removed for the world, and most importantly for us, to discover who we truly are. While we are not responsible for our early conditioning, including trauma, we, too, have helped build much of our mind-made prisons through our habits, beliefs, and the information we have consumed. These have all been reinforced by the fact that most of us really believe the stories we tell ourselves. When we provide ourselves with self-talk containing the same information and reinforce it repeatedly with consistent narratives, we create a brain circuitry capable of believing and acting from a very limited point of view.

This reminds me of an anecdote attributed to various Native American traditions. A great elder was asked one day, "Inside of me are two dogs. One dog is mean and evil. The other dog is good. The mean dog battles the good dog constantly." When the wise elder is asked which dog triumphs, he paused for a moment before mindfully responding, "The one I feed the most."

The story presents a simple but powerful metaphor for the dangers of consistently 'feeding' ourselves with certain dogmas, philosophies, and information without being aware of how these doctrines are moving us in the direction of the content we are providing. Here, the two dogs represent the dualistic nature of our choices in life. The 'mean or evil' dog embodies our negative and limiting thoughts, beliefs, habits, fears, self-talk, and information (including certain news networks and social media). These all have the capacity to build highly restrictive tiny prison cells. Conversely, the 'good or mindful' dog represents awareness and openness that leads to happiness, positive emotions, and actions such as love, kindness, joy, empathy, and generosity.

**The Layers of Debris**

Let's briefly dissect the layers of debris that obscure our true *Selves*, starting with our beliefs. I cannot recall a time when it has been more evident that many of us perceive life through restrictive and polarizing lenses or labels. You may identify as a conservative or a liberal, a Democrat or a Republican, a Christian, Muslim, Buddhist, Hindu, or Jew. The labels we assign ourselves typically bias our perception of reality and are intrinsically linked to many other beliefs.

As I write this, I'm returning to Arizona after our traditional 4th of July week at Myrtle Beach. The week of the 4th, the beach was filled with hundreds of flags representing various belief systems. On the last evening of my trip, I noticed a stir around a dozen flags planted about 100 yards down the beach. Initially, I thought this was a heartening display of unity, various groups bridging their differences by bringing diverse perspectives together. As I approached, I saw the stark opposite - an agitated gathering, their flags emblematic of some disturbing and hateful viewpoints.

The group's leader wore a T-shirt that read, "Don't waste ammunition. Kill them the first time with a 9mm." As a follower of Jesus's teachings, I was deeply disturbed to see, amidst those flags, a Christian flag bearing a cross. I struggle to reconcile sentiments represented by the flags and tee shirts with Jesus's teachings in the Sermon on the Mount (Matthew 5:38-41), "You have heard that it was said, 'Eye for eye, and tooth for tooth.' But I tell you, do not resist an evil person. If anyone slaps you on the right cheek, turn to them the other cheek also. And if anyone wants to sue you and take your shirt, hand over your coat as well. If anyone forces you to go one mile, go with them two miles." These words are immediately followed by verses urging love for one's enemies. How could these direct messages be so flagrantly misinterpreted and merged with hateful rhetoric?

Yet, therein lies the danger of such beliefs. Sacred truths, such as the principles of non-violence, going the extra mile for others, and loving one's enemies, can be hijacked and twisted by a malignant belief system. When such distortions are propagated as exclusive truths, and those who dissent are deemed lesser or threatening to the cause, a dangerous mixture is formed. This volatile concoction fosters tribalism and extremism, justifying even the most abhorrent actions. History has illuminated this truth across many religions, where one religion's martyr is often seen as a terrorist by another.

A second similar layer involves our ideas, especially those concerning people. If we hold a rigid idea about someone or some group, that clouds our perception of who they truly are. This person or group could say or do something or behave in a certain way, and we quickly label them based on our preconceived notions. Consequently, whenever we come in contact with them next, we interact not with the person or group but with the idea we have of them.

A third layer is anchored in our habits. Certain habits, like walking and driving, are vital for daily functioning. Yet, it's crucial to discern which habits should be confined to mechanical actions and which should not encroach upon feelings like love or appreciation of beauty. As I previously mentioned, aside from the flag incident, I've just returned from a glorious week at the beach. As a self-proclaimed 'beach person', I cherish every aspect of the beach, from the feeling of warm sand sifting through my toes, the soothing caress of the cool sea breeze, the rhythmic ebb and flow of the waves, the distant cries of seagulls, the laughter of children, and the view of the setting sun as the sky explodes into hues of pink, orange, and purple.

However, as much as I love the beach, I wonder if I were a fisherman looking at the ocean daily, would the habitual exposure cause a numbing effect? Would I lose my ability to recognize its magnificence due to my constant contact with it? Often, we form fixed ideas about all the things we see, and when we encounter them, we don't experience their ever-changing freshness in the present moment. Instead, we see the same dull, recycled idea molded in our minds that were produced by habit. This habitual perception infiltrates how we interact with people and things, causing a lack of freshness and creativity and leading to mechanical and routine interactions.

The fourth highly influential layer pertains to our fear and early childhood conditioning and trauma. That's why I focused the entire previous chapter on these vital issues.

The last layer I want to discuss in this chapter focuses on the impact of our self-talk on how we view our lives. As I have said throughout this book, We believe the stories we tell ourselves, so be very careful what you tell yourself. What we tell ourselves creates a layer within us that produces our self-perception and becomes a key factor in determining the size of our prison cells. I love the quote by Bruce Lee, a Hong Kong-American actor, director, and considered one of the greatest martial artists of all time. "Don't speak negatively about yourself, even as a joke. Your body doesn't know the difference. Words are energy and cast spells... Change how you speak of yourself, and you can change your life."

This quote embodies the incredible power of negative self-talk. When Lee says, "Don't speak negatively about yourself, even as a joke," he's highlighting the idea that our minds often can't distinguish between what's said in jest and what's serious or whether it is being said by us or someone else. This blurring of lines can cause even lighthearted self-deprecation to infuse our subconscious with negative perceptions about ourselves.

His statement, "Words are energy and cast spells," reveals that our words aren't just a tool for communication but a force that shapes our reality. The 'spells' we cast with our words, especially about ourselves, manifest in our self-image, impacting our actions, decisions, and overall outlook. Again, with self-talk, we determine the size of our mind-made prison cells. By altering our self-talk from negative to positive, we don't just tweak our mindset but effectively transform our lives. When we talk positively about ourselves, we start perceiving ourselves more favorably, bolstering our confidence, breaking down the prison cell walls, and uncovering the happiness within us.

Each layer serves as a reminder that we're all navigating life through our unique perceptual filters, heavily influenced by our beliefs, ideas, habits, early conditioning, attachments, and fears. Becoming aware of these layers is the first step towards better understanding ourselves and our interactions with the world around us.

**Why I Can't Tell the Truth**

I have recently had to come to terms with the fact that no matter how hard I try, sometimes I just can't remember things as they actually happened. This inaccurate remembering can play a key role in the shape and size of our mind-made prisons. Progressive Insurance has a hilarious set of commercials in which a couple throws a football replay challenge flag on the field, just like in NFL football when a coach wants to dispute a referee's call on an important football play. The referee then comes into the couple's homes, plays the replay, and settles common household disagreements.

The campaign is very funny because of how true it is. We all have moments in life we wish we could go back and review to settle a disagreement. The first commercial spot features a couple unloading a canoe from their car near a river when they realize they have left their life jackets at home. This, of course, leads to a game of 'he said, she said'. With the challenge flag thrown, a replay official appears to end the finger-pointing and confirm who was correct all along.

We can all agree that real life might benefit from challenge flags. Just imagine how many times this has happened in your life and how many arguments we'd be able to settle if we could just go back to a tape and confirm who did or did not say what. One of our biggest relational issues is determining the truth in certain critical situations.

I know for me this has happened in all my relationships. I can't remember the number of times when I've asked myself if my wife or a friend really believe what they're saying. But perhaps I don't remember a correct version of the truth. Are we both just dishonest liars trying to win an argument or make our point or is there something more fundamental about our memories that can become distorted and make them false?

In trying to understand all of this, it is critical to remember that our memories are assembled and encoded when we construct and retrieve the memories. We do not store photographic images of our memories, of what is actually happening in our world, but instead, we encode and store our own personal interpretations and feelings of the memory, and that is all based on past experiences, fears, transference (of past memories), and our perspective at the time.

Later, when asked what happened, we reconstruct the experience based on the information we retrieve from our original memory and what we might infer given our current expectations and perspective, which have likely changed from the first time we stored the memory. We then restore a reconstructed version of the experience, which is highly likely to be a more modified or distorted version of what originally happened.

More recent memories, when retrieved, are more likely to be true to the original and somewhat resistant to change. However, as our monkey minds replay or loop a particularly disturbing event or dispute, especially with a loved one or partner, the truth is often distorted more with each loop. Loop that memory several times in an evening, and you can imagine how that impacts the validity of the memory and your perspective on it. This is why it is vital at times like these that we exercise humility, especially in our capacity to remember important events that are likely to cause conflict.

Understanding that older memories are more subject to distortion is also critical. Details may have faded over time, although the gist of the memory may remain. The self-conception may have evolved or regressed, and the old memory has had a great capacity to be reinterpreted in terms of our present self, new information, new fears, and a new context.

Obviously, this adds an important level of complexity to our and others' memories. It also lets us know that how someone remembers something may be highly associated with their background traumas, fears, perspectives, and level of consciousness. It's almost hard to imagine how we live in a world with so much possibility of impreciseness when it comes to memories. I find it amazing not that we don't get along but that we love each other despite all of this crazy-making.

If we keep telling the same wrong story over and over, we are building the very brain circuitry that will never allow us to see an event the way it truly happened. More importantly, this allows us to justify destructive decisions that can impact us for the rest of our lives. Once again, awareness that this is happening is the key to somewhat overcoming it. Once I realized that no matter how much I believed a story to be true, it had the great capacity to be false or at least altered by exaggeration, the humbler I became about the absolute validity of my memories and their capacity to lead me in a good direction. Now, as I sit in my CAST meditations, my *I* can look at disturbing memories and not attach to them, but simply be curious about them. The *I* in me will ask itself, I wonder why I keep recalling that memory and why it is bothering me so much. At that point, I'm much more apt to see this as a problem within me and not a problem with someone else.

**It's Time for a Prison Break**

As I reflect on all my past attempts at self-improvement, most have ended in disappointment, or if they did succeed, it was only a small change for a little while. Now, imagine if you ceased striving to change yourself and stopped all dissatisfaction with who you are. Would this lead to a passive acceptance of everything within and around you? Is there no alternative between laborious self-pushing and stagnant acceptance? Indeed, *there is another way*, and that centers around awareness and self-understanding.

This, however, is no easy journey. To truly understand who you are demands complete freedom from all desires to transform yourself into something different. Instead of attempting to change, strive to observe. Study your reactions to people and things without judgment or condemnation, and all desires to reform yourself will cease.

Let your observations remain fluid, free from rigid conclusions, and open to fresh perspectives from one moment to the next. You'll then witness a marvelous transformation within you. You will be flooded with the light of awareness, and this transparency will enable transformation. Change will occur within you and around you, but it won't be instigated by the restless ego that constantly competes, compares, and generates tension, conflict, and resistance between you and the world around you.

This new way will produce change that is not forced or artificial. Instead, it will be a natural, organic process rooted in increased self-awareness and understanding. The transformative power of self-observation is immense and can unlock a profound sense of peace and contentment within you.

*It is time for a prison break!*

How do we break out of our tiny prison cells? First, realize that the prison walls were built around us for one major reason: our minds have fallen asleep. We don't see this, so we live and die as prison inmates. Most people conform and adapt to prison life. There are a few who become reformers, advocating for better prison conditions. However, rarely do we become revolutionaries, ready to completely break down the prison walls. To be a revolutionary, we must first recognize that we have built this mind-made prison that we find ourselves in.

Secondly, we must spend time contemplating the structure of these walls. What are they made of? Observe your ideas, habits, attachments, self-talk, stories, and fears, without judgment or condemnation. Look at them, become aware of all their contours, and they will crumble.

Thirdly, spend time observing the things and people around you. Look at a friend's face, a leaf, a tree, a bird in flight, the behavior and mannerisms of people around you as if for the very first time. Really see them, hopefully anew, free from the dulling effect of your ideas and habits.

And the most crucial step is to sit quietly in meditation and observe how your mind functions. This is the second chapter in the second step- "Deepening **A**wareness." Become aware of the steady flow of thoughts, feelings, and reactions moving through your mind. Watch this flow for long stretches of time, the way you would watch a river or a movie. If you are really curious, you'll find them more absorbing than any movie, more life-giving, and liberating. After all, can we be said to be alive if we aren't even aware of our thoughts and reactions? Without such awareness, there is no freedom; it cannot even be called life. It's a mechanical existence of constantly living with our unconscious *Me*. So, watch, observe, question, explore, deepen your awareness, and your mind will awaken, shed all of its layers, and become alert and active. *Then, magically, your prison walls will tumble down, and you will be free at last!*

# Chapter 6 - Loneliness

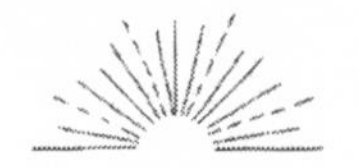

In my previous book, *The Rewired Brain*[5], I had a humbling and almost show-stopping moment while preparing to pen a chapter I had titled "What It Means to be Human" in my original book proposal. Who did I think I was, indeed, daring to encapsulate such an enormous concept within the constraints of a mere chapter? The complexity and overwhelming nature of the endeavor tormented me, and for nearly a month, I struggled to place even a single word on paper.

On one particular morning, after weeks of grueling introspection, my answer came from a very unexpected place. My shower routine had been the same for years; as the warm water pours, I fill my home with the sweet, soulful strains of Motown, a musical tradition inherited from my father. Growing up, my evenings were filled with the beats and ballads of The Temptations, Diana Ross, and Marvin Gaye - artists my father revered as keepers and whisperers of unvarnished human emotion. Despite our humble tobacco farm upbringing in rural North Carolina, through the power of music, we could taste a slice of the vibrant culture that thrived a world away in Detroit.

I remember my father often remarked, "Ski, soul artists sing about their feelings. They show you what's in their hearts. And they tell you the truth about life." These words remain nestled in my heart and still play out in my mornings' routine. The music has always provided incredible beauty and passion that can soothe my impending challenges of the day.

On this particularly challenging morning, while wrestling with the first word of my chapter, the chorus of a 1974 song from one of my father's favorite Motown groups, The Main Ingredient, played in the background: "I just don't want to be lonely" as I grappled with the daunting question from my book—"What does it mean to be human?" By the third refrain of the song's pivotal line, as the volume of the song appeared to increase each time, I found myself, toothbrush in hand, staring at my reflection in the mirror. Suddenly, the epiphany struck. As the soulful melody of the song amplified, it eventually overcame my intricate introspection on the topic. I recall exclaiming aloud, "That's it!" To be human is to grapple with our loneliness, our excruciating isolation, our yearning to connect, and our fearful journey toward the conclusion of our known existence.

My dad passed away from cancer far too early, at 66, and I miss him deeply. Yet, I believe that he, on that day eight years ago, somehow reached out through the veil of his current existence to provide me with the answer to the profound question of what it means to be human.

**Another Unbearable Prison**

If my experience means anything, a critical part of being human is wrestling with the torment of isolation, craving relationships, and undertaking the often disastrous quest to soothe our loneliness. This revelation was partly influenced by the works of Erich Fromm, whose theories have had a profound impact on me.

Erich Fromm (1900 – 1980) was a German social psychologist, psychoanalyst, sociologist, and humanistic philosopher. He immigrated from Germany to the United States in 1934, escaping the Nazi regime, and held various academic positions in prestigious institutions such as Columbia University, Yale University, and Michigan State University.

Some of Fromm's most influential works include *Escape from Freedom*[13] and *The Art of Loving*[14]. In these, he explores themes of freedom, love, and identity, examining how they are intertwined within societal structures and individual mental health. Fromm proposed that love is an art. Fromm advocated for the capacity and freedom each individual possesses to induce self-change and govern their lives. Yet, like this book, he acknowledged that fear often prevents us from embracing this potential.

Regarding loneliness, Fromm wrote, "This awareness of himself as a separate entity, the awareness of his own short life span, of the fact that without his will he is born and against his will, he dies, that he will die before those whom he loves, or they before him, the awareness of his aloneness and separateness, of his helplessness before the forces of nature and of society, all this makes his separate, disunited existence an unbearable prison."

From Fromm's perspective, loneliness was more than a state of being alone. It is a deeply rooted psychological condition stemming from isolation, separateness, and disconnectedness. This, in turn, has an incredible propensity to fuel overwhelming anxiety and despair.

Fromm championed love, not as a transient emotion but as a beautiful interpersonal form of art, as the antidote to existential loneliness. Through genuine love, he maintained that we have the potential to bridge the chasm of separateness, move past our individual isolation, and diminish the ache of loneliness. Fromm saw love as the remedy for human loneliness. As you will discover at the end of this chapter, I believe love is the ultimate solution to our loneliness, and only love gives us the unique capacity to be truly human.

**Modern Loneliness**

But for now, one does not have to look far for evidence of loneliness in Western societies such as the US. First, we are seeing an epidemic of mental health disorders, including depression and anxiety. These disorders are directly associated with loneliness, each one fueling the other in an awful, negative cycle.

Additionally, statistics reveal that more people than ever are living alone. According to the 2019 U.S. Census Bureau data, approximately 28% of households have just one person. We are seeing trends like these as marriage rates have steadily declined in Western societies. Clearly, many factors come into play here, but it seems that we are becoming less inclined to form deep, intimate connections.

Of course, the big one is our growing attachment to technology. While it may appear to keep us connected, much of this is merely an illusion of connection. There's a strange paradox at play when we look at social media. You'd think that with these incredible tools, feelings of loneliness would be on the decline. But social psychology research paints a different picture. In fact, the more time we are connected digitally, the lonelier we become.

Why? There are many reasons. For example, when we find ourselves in a world where we can instantly observe the lives of others, we often quite deceptively see a world filled with pictures of perfection. Now, we all know these are typically meticulously crafted illusions of how others want us to see them. They are not reality. And yet, we can't help measuring our lives against the unrealistic standards we see on our screens. This generates a deep sense of inadequacy, and we feel more disconnected than ever because we don't believe we measure up.

Now, don't get me wrong. Social media has several important perks, as it can bridge geographical gaps, allowing us to maintain ties with family and friends who are far away. It can introduce new perspectives and ideas, expanding our understanding of the world.

However, as I think of the lessons we learned from the COVID-19 pandemic, perhaps the biggest one is we simply can't replace genuine, face-to-face human interaction—the kind that involves body language, tone of voice, and physical touch. Virtual connections simply can't, nor will they ever be able to replicate the depth and warmth of intimate relationships.

Importantly, there are also much darker sides to these platforms. Cyberbullying is an incredibly damaging form of abuse. It breaks my heart that it is so prevalent among our youth as it inflicts deep emotional wounds and leads to feelings of loneliness, isolation, and even suicide.

And lastly, it is the silent thief of our time. I'm blown away at the number of times I feel like I have spent only a few minutes of mindless scrolling. Then, I look at my watch, and it's been an hour. How does time move so quickly when we are scrolling?

This is such an insidious loss of our precious moments. Much of this book focuses on the importance of being in the present moment. And yet, we waste our moments and lives so effortlessly. This is the only time you will ever have this present moment again. In the end, we are left feeling empty and unfulfilled, further contributing to our sense of loneliness.

**We Are All Dying**

Did I get your attention? I think this may be the most overlooked and obvious aspect of our human existence. And yet, the dying process starts the moment we are born. What's more, our lifetimes here are so very short. However, we appear incapable of facing this vital facet as we live obliviously until it is thrust upon us. I think this is because it can be so frightening and mysterious, and in the end, we must do it alone. This is clearly echoed in Fromm's earlier quote. "The awareness of his own short life span, of the fact that without his will he is born and against his will, he dies, that he will die before those whom he loves, or they before him… his helplessness before the forces of nature…makes his separate, disunited existence an unbearable prison." I wrote in the last chapter about the prison cells we build for ourselves, but the one Fromm speaks of here is imposed upon us.

I have had three cancer scares. The first was a softball size tumor on my spine, found not to be a deadly osteosarcoma as the doctors originally thought, but an extremely rare bone-forming tumor that can become locally aggressive but was unlikely to kill me. This experience was my first dress rehearsal for considering cancer and death. It profoundly changed me. I would get the opportunity to use this experience over the next 15 years, as two additional types of real cancers would become a part of my future.

I vividly remember that first diagnosis. I freaked out. There was the feeling that all the blood and oxygen had left my body, similar to the ensuing numbness of tightly clinching your hand. My *Me* was going crazy, as the same thoughts looped incessantly through my mind as the sensation of pressure accumulated in my chest around the area of my heart. It seemed unimaginable and incredibly frightening that *I* and *Me* would cease to exist and leave my four children behind. What about all the experiences I would miss? Who would give my daughters away at their weddings, cuddle and praise my future grandchildren; and watch football with my boys on Sundays? The thought of these absences took my breath away as I found myself in the middle of my worst nightmare. All at once, I realized that my family, friends, and life—despite being very short—were incredibly precious to me and not something I could envision losing. And yet, as I write this, I am still surprised that I had not considered dying before. Somehow, the thought of it must be too hard for most of us to consider until it is forced upon us.

Why is it so hard for us to face our mortality, and why does it produce such loneliness? In Chapter 2, I described how survival is the primary objective of our unconscious *Me.* Now imagine what happens when survival is instantly placed at grave risk by a frightening cancer diagnosis. Our *Me* goes crazy and creates the most intense, unconscious emotions and feelings, generating extreme conscious stress and anxiety. Our unconscious minds leap towards worst-case scenario narratives. That resulted in the complete freak out I was experiencing with my first cancer experience. My *Me* would not rest while replaying the same terrifying and depressing thoughts and feelings at a thousand miles an hour. I believe this is exactly what Fromm was describing when he used the term, "an unbearable prison."

I will leave you here with a cliffhanger; I will detail my beliefs about life, death, and eternity in the book's last chapter, "Embracing the

Unknowables". No surprise, it will involve our *I* and its connection to the Divine. But for now, I simply want to validate those who are going or have gone through similar or even worse experiences and make us all aware of the intense loneliness that facing our mortality can generate.

**Messed Up**

As a scientist, I find that the vast mysteries of our existence are outside of the reach of the scientific method. Then, I find myself looking inward to experience a world without form. As evidenced by this book, I have been drawn to my spiritual nature. With it, I believe I can connect with Divine wisdom to better understand the universe and my role in it. This understanding is vital, individually and collectively, as our Divine-like consciousnesses have great creativity to imagine and act.

This almost implausible capacity is also accompanied by a destructive power that currently threatens our planet and the extinction of thousands of species, including us. However, I believe the conscious *I* also allows us to partner and co-create with the Divine to prevent suffering, improve— and maybe even save— creation. I first recognized this co-creative responsibility on my first trip to Africa.

I have always been mesmerized by the continent of Africa. Even before I first went there, my scientific understanding had revealed it to be the cradle of humanity. I instinctively knew that a trip there would allow me to sense the essential heartbeat of humanity. That first trip came almost eighteen years ago during a particularly difficult period of my life. A charitable organization organized the trip at a time when HIV/AIDS had wiped out large numbers of young parents. After 30 long hours of travel by air and van, I found myself in South Africa, at a small Bible college, surrounded by a 15-foot-high barbed wire fence in the middle of a very large shantytown called Masoyi. We brought with us food, water, shoes, and deworming medications for thousands of orphans. Masoyi consisted of shacks made of plywood, corrugated metal, sheets of plastic, and cardboard boxes.

Following a few hours of sleep, we were welcomed with a hearty breakfast and a devotional by Manny Ohonme. Manny had left Nigeria to play college basketball in the US. He had since become a successful businessman and was now CEO of a non-profit organization, Samaritan's Feet International. He was a huge man, and his smile was even bigger and infectious.

After the devotional, Manny spotted me in the corner, approached me, looked me in the eye, and said, "My new friend, you are about to be messed up!" Taken aback, I stared at him as if he were crazy. I had no idea what he meant by his bold statement. And then, Mr. Lizard Brain began to shout inside my head, "Obviously, he does not know who you are. You are a famous scientist. You've got it all together. You can't mess me up!" But two days later, that's exactly what happened.

While visiting a banana plantation where hundreds of orphaned children were housed behind a barbed wire fence, I encountered a child who would forever change my life. When we first stepped off the van at the plantation, I immediately saw older children sticking their heads through the sharp coils to look at us "rich" Americans. However, off in one corner of the lot was a group of about fifty infants and young children sitting in muddy, parasite-infested sewer water. Some were playing, others splashing, but most were crying, wailing at the top of their lungs. I don't know why, but I was drawn to one of those children. He was about 2 years old and so very ill. Due to AIDS and tuberculosis, he was experiencing liver failure, and his eyes were deep yellow. His face was distorted due to a birth defect, disease, and malnutrition. He was so weak he could only cry halfheartedly. I wanted to know his name. But the 'granny,' an older woman in charge of all the small children, shook her head; she did not know. I realized these children did not have names. This thought took my breath away and completely broke my heart.

As I stared at the weakly crying baby, I wanted to hold him, but I also knew that to be a great risk. He had fluid seeping from all parts of his body, and there was a good probability of contracting a disease (AIDS or drug-resistant TB) that I knew could kill me. But somehow, I knew I had to. I kept hearing what I now believe from my *I*, "Pick that child up, please." I did as instructed and picked the child up from the muddy water, wiped his face with my shirt, and pressed his face against mine. Holding his emaciated body tight, I softly sang the same lullaby my mom had sung to me. "Bye, oh baby, oh bye, oh baby." The little guy immediately stopped crying and looked into my eyes. For the first time, I perceived that I was looking into the precious eyes of God. My perspective about almost everything dissolved, and a new purpose arrived in its place.

At that moment, for the first time in my life, I felt a powerful yearning. Standing there, staring at a malnourished, crying baby in the sweltering African heat, I sensed from the Divine two questions: "Who are you?" and "Whose are you?" Spiritually and professionally, I believe those two questions changed my life forever.

"Who was I?" I believe this sacred ground and the questions reminded me of my connection to humanity. I was spiritually linked to this child through the family of humanity in ways I could not even comprehend. In showing love to this child and others, I realized that I was showing God's love to the entire human race, including myself.

The question "Whose are you?" prompted me to step up to a life of action that moved well beyond mere words, theology, my religious traditions, or even spirituality. I instantly knew that I had a responsibility to provide unconditional love to all inhabitants of this earth.

My new best friend Manny was right when he said I was about to be "messed up" in the most beautiful and meaningful way possible. But now I could see everything in a different way. It will take me several lifetimes to perfect this highest of all calls. But even if I'm not perfect, I somehow realized that if I tried, the universe and its Purposeful Designer would accept me as a partner, dare I say co-creator, and by fulfilling this sacred mission, I would receive immense love in return.

This deeply resonated with the writings of Fromm discussed at the beginning of this chapter. As you may remember, Fromm advocated the transformative nature of love—not as a fleeting feeling but as a continuous, powerful force that has the power to counter the existential fear of loneliness and even death. With this profound form of love, we can span the void of isolation, live in personal stillness, and approach the end of our lives without the stinging pain of loneliness. This was a profound *awakening* for me, a critical step towards walking out of the prison cell of my unconscious *Me*.

Since that moment, eighteen years ago, I have participated in nonprofit organizations throughout the U.S. and Africa. As discussed in Chapter 4, I am now part of a non-profit that brings crisis relief, education, and hope to victims of civil war, genocide, and religious persecution within Sudan.

While my *Me* thinks this is all very impressive and wants to brag, my conscious true *Self*, my *I*, realizes that I needed and still need Africa so much more than Africa needs me. Africa is where I understood my sacred responsibility and the restorative power of love, which allows us to co-create, to partner with the Divine.

# Step 3 -

# The Art of <u>S</u>urrender

In the prior chapters of Step 2 - Deepening **<u>A</u>**wareness, I intended to help us unearth the self-imposed mental confines and the traumatic experiences that have lurked in the recesses of our minds, governing our lives in ways we could not fully understand. This process required peeling back layers of our unconscious *Me*, digging through memories, and sometimes facing painful realities that we'd much rather forget. Yet, this discovery and increased awareness process is a crucial and, at times, an extremely painful part of our journey.

As we transition into Step 3 - The Art of **<u>S</u>**urrender, we're evolving to another stage of insight. In life, we often find ourselves trying to grasp tightly onto moments, people, or things, attempting to solidify them in our reality. Yet, our world is in constant flux, ever-changing, and ever-evolving. This is the nature of existence. Although challenging, recognizing and accepting this truth is a crucial step toward peace and fulfillment. When we accept and surrender to the impermanence of life, we let go of our rigid expectations and the illusion of control. We begin to flow with life's ebb and tide rather than resist it, finding beauty and wisdom in life's transient moments. Importantly, we begin to understand that it is often during our most difficult and painful experiences that we grow into the beings we were meant to be.

Surrender is not about giving up but about understanding that we cannot force life to conform to our desires. It's about allowing life to unfold naturally, trusting in the process, and finding serenity amid constant change. With each breath and heartbeat, we live in a cycle of impermanence; it's when we accept and surrender to this truth that we truly begin to live.

It's also time to bravely examine and surrender the many beliefs, ideas, habits, negative self-talk, fears, and early conditioning, including trauma that we may harbor in our unconscious minds. In certain instances, the origins of these feelings might have been so severe, so indescribably painful, that they're buried deep within, hidden away in a subconscious vault far beyond our immediate access. Yet, whether we consciously remember these instances or not, they birth emotions and feelings that breed thousands of destructive thoughts and reactions.

Step 3 can, at times, seem incredibly challenging, but remember, with the increasing awareness we have gained in Steps 1 and 2, we find ourselves equipped to observe our minds and let go of everything that has stunted our growth and covered our innate happiness. By now, we are starting to discern whether our thoughts are inadvertently sowing seeds of struggle or if we're intentionally allowing them to do so. We are beginning to comprehend how excruciating it can be to resist the present moment or battle with past events that are no longer within our control.

We must now embrace the great Swiss psychiatrist/psychoanalyst Carl Jung's words, "What you resist, persists", as we understand that denying or resisting aspects of our subconscious mind will only make those elements more pronounced. Resisting directly empowers the very things we are trying to escape. Instead, we powerfully move toward inner peace when we acknowledge, confront, and let go of these feelings and emotions.

The two chapters within Step 3 serve as guides, gently leading us toward an understanding that acceptance, surrender, and letting go of our desperate attempts to control or resist difficult situations is the key to uncovering our innate happiness. This state of non-resistance creates a mental and emotional space free of conflict and confusion.

From this newfound perspective, the bushel basket that has obscured the light of inherent happiness is finally lifted. We are then left with an unobstructed view of our inner joy, which radiates outward, transforming our lives and the lives of others in ways we never thought possible. In my opinion, the transformation that surrender brings is the most sacred, deeply personal, and undeniably freeing Step of the four in this book. Through the Art of **S**urrender, we will find our pathway to peace and contentment, no longer shadowed by the heavy clouds of our past or present conflicts or future worries.

# Chapter 7 -

# Wild Fires and New Beginnings

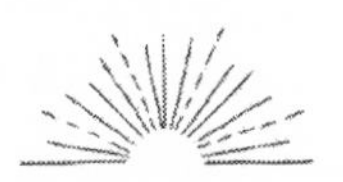

### The Wisdom of the Sonoran Desert

I'll never forget sitting in a field at dusk near my home in Tucson, Arizona, watching an entire mountain range burn. The Bighorn Fire in the 9,000-foot Catalina Mountains started with several lightning strikes in the summer of 2020 and consumed almost 120,000 acres before it was finally contained. This was my first full summer living in Arizona, and while I had heard of these fires, what I had read or been told did not begin to describe what I was witnessing.

I cried as I watched, oscillating between gazing at the towering inferno and covering my eyes to avoid the sight. After living in the Sonoran Desert for only a year, this magnificent desert, with its incredibly diverse ecosystem, and particularly this mountain range, had come to mean everything to me. It was home to grand geological wonders and many miraculous plants and animals. I loved the trails that I hiked every weekend.

Being a biology nerd, I couldn't wrap my head around the fact that this was one of the hottest deserts on earth and, at the same time, one of the most biodiverse in the world. How was that possible? How could two brief rainy seasons, contrasted with little or no water the rest of the year and temperatures as high as 115 degrees in the summer, produce such plant and animal diversity?

I found the desert untamed and wild, with a wide array of creatures. There are the desert bighorn sheep, coyotes, javelinas, and the Sonoran pronghorn. Various reptiles reside here, including the Sonoran Desert Tortoise and a unique assortment of lizards and snakes. The birds, including roadrunners, cactus wrens, owls, and hawks, are everywhere. I even relished encountering the occasional Western Diamondback Rattlesnake, one of the largest rattlesnake species in the world. If I was truly lucky, as has happened only three times in five years, I would get to see a Gila Monster. The Gila Monster, one of only two venomous lizard species in the world and native to the Sonoran Desert, has vibrant skin—a black body with orange patches, a bright pattern with an almost beaded appearance. Experiencing it transported me back 200 million years to when dinosaurs roamed the earth.

And then there were the majestic plants. These included the Palo Verde, with its green "verde" trunk and branches, providing shelter and food for numerous animal species. I had never experienced a sweeter smell than that of Creosote bushes after a desert rain. But my favorites are the cacti. These included the Prickly Pear, the Organ Pipe, and the insidious Cholla Cactus known to "jump" and assail passers, including myself, with thousands of spines.

However, my very favorite regal being in the entire desert is the Saguaro Cactus. The only place on earth where this magnificent cactus grows is the Sonoran Desert. It seemed to me to defy all the laws of nature. It lives 150 to 200 years and grows as high as 60 feet tall. That's equivalent to a six-story building! One of the distinguishing features of the Saguaro is its arms; these usually start growing after the cactus reaches about 15 feet in height and around 75 years of age.

In the spring, Saguaros burst forth with crowns of large, creamy white flowers, which only bloom at night. These flowers are pollinated by bats, birds, and insects and produce red and fleshy fruits enjoyed by a variety of desert animals and traditionally harvested by Native Americans for food. The Saguaros also provide vital habitats for desert birds such as Gila woodpeckers and purple martins. Even in death, a Saguaro serves its ecosystem, with its woody ribs providing building materials and fuel to Native Americans. I have never encountered a more noble, grand, generous, and dare I say, loving being. Is there any wonder this magnificent desert captured this North Carolina boy's heart?

And now, with this massive fire, it was all gone. The destruction before me broke my heart. When I was finally able to return a month later, there was little left of the beautiful plants, cacti, and trees that I had so cherished. I wondered about all the animals—where had they gone? Did they make it out alive?

Little did I know at the time, but this desert, with its knowing Saguaro Cactus, held another crucial piece of ancient wisdom to impart.

Despite the devastation, I wasn't prepared to abandon the desert, so I continued my weekend hikes. To my astonishment, I began to notice a remarkable transformation. Plants started to return—the small, fast-growing species appeared first, followed by slower-growing bushes. I gradually realized that my beloved playground was a habitat designed to evolve in the wake of regular wildfires. In fact, the wildfires were crucial to the desert ecosystem, shaping its biological diversity.

These fires, for instance, release nutrients back into the soil, enhancing the nutrient cycling process supporting a broader range of plant species. Many plants, particularly certain types of desert cacti and wildflowers, have seeds that require the heat of a wildfire or the post-fire conditions to germinate. These plants then rapidly recolonize the area, contributing to overall plant diversity.

Wildfires also alter habitats in ways that favor certain species. For example, they clear out dominant vegetation, allowing less common, fire-adapted species to flourish. Often, wildfires can control invasive plant species that aren't adapted to fire, providing room for native plant species to thrive.

Additionally, wildfires can increase food availability. For instance, the new growth that follows a fire can provide an abundance of food for herbivores, which, in turn, indirectly supports a greater diversity of predators.

My purpose in writing this isn't to provide a biology lesson or even describe my profound love for my new Sonoran Desert home. It is to share what I believe to be another crucial first principle for life. Just like the desert, the wildfires in our lives are necessary to pave the way for beautiful new beginnings. When I mentioned that "many plants, especially certain types of desert cacti and wildflowers have seeds that require the heat of a fire or the post-fire conditions in order to germinate," I believe the same applies to humans. When I said that "fires clear out dominant vegetation, allowing less common, fire-adapted species to increase in abundance," I believe the same is true for humans. And when I wrote that "the new growth that follows a fire can provide an abundance," I believe the same applies to humans.

I firmly believe that the painful cycles of symbolic wildfires in our lives are designed to generate beautiful new beginnings. You see, this desert with its knowing Saguaro Cactus had much to teach me.

**Impermanence and the "Law of Undulation"**

In Western cultures, we typically resist the idea of change. We place a very high value on stability and predictability and aim for steadiness across almost all aspects of our lives—our jobs, institutions, relationships, and possessions. The notion that we could lose everything—our jobs, possessions, and even our lives (as discussed in the previous chapter)—strikes fear in our hearts. As a result, we make plans, hold meetings, appoint committees, nominate boards, and read self-help books, all in an effort not just to maintain but to grow and enrich these things.

We form strong attachments to people, roles, and possessions, and the thought of losing them preoccupies most of our waking hours. As I write this book, isolated in a beach community in Mexico, I recall three

Americans who approached me just yesterday. Their primary complaint? They couldn't believe how much the US has changed and, in their view, how it is 'going to hell' so rapidly. For them, change represented the worst possible outcome. And even when things aren't changing for people, there seems to be a desperate need to pretend they are and then fear their own illusions.

Think this doesn't apply to you? Consider your habits. Do you hoard things? Are your closets overflowing? How about your garage? Do you even have a storage unit? And what about your perspective on change? Are you fixated on it, talking about it constantly? Do you view it negatively?

Recently, I had the opportunity to help dispose of a deceased person's possessions. Everything in the house had its own spot. There were closets and a garage filled to the brim with pictures, knick-knacks, junk, and furniture. We found ourselves with nowhere to put it all. After three days of trying to decide where it should go or who should inherit it, we were desperate. Goodwill and the Salvation Army accepted a few things, but the rest went to the dump. Most of this elderly person's lifetime possessions ended up in the trash. It may sound crass, but she went into the grave, and her stuff went into the garbage.

What if we could give up our need for stability and predictability for things to remain unchanged? Do you think we would be happier and more at peace?

In Eastern spirituality, this concept has transformed my Western ideas of stability and, in turn, my life. It is called impermanence. Impermanence was a fundamental principle of the Buddha's teachings. It refers to the fact that all physical and mental phenomena are in a constant state of change. Nothing is exempt; this is a fundamental law of nature, another first principle, if you will.

Buddhist thought teaches that understanding impermanence isn't just about acknowledging the reality of physical decay and death but also about recognizing the changing nature of all experiences, emotions, perceptions, and mental formations. From moment to moment, things arise, and things pass away. As you will see later in the book, this is a central tenet on which much of mindful meditation is based.

The Buddha taught that understanding impermanence was the key to liberation. Suffering arises not from the fact that everything changes but from attachment and clinging to the idea that people, possessions, experiences, and even our concept of self will not change. By fully realizing the impermanent nature of all things, we can reduce our cravings and thus diminish our suffering.

Just to be clear, this isn't meant to create a pessimistic worldview. Instead, it's meant to cultivate a deep understanding of how things really are. Accepting this wisdom provides greater peace, freedom, and compassion. As we let go of clinging to all aspects of our lives, including our life itself, we can enjoy and bask in the present moment.

C.S. Lewis introduced a similar concept called the "Law of Undulation" in his book, *The Screwtape Letters*[15]. The book is written as a series of letters from a senior demon, Screwtape, to his nephew Wormwood, advising him on how best to lead his assigned humans into sin and away from God. Despite the unusual concept, this is one of the most important books I have ever read.

The "Law of Undulation" refers to the natural ebb and flow of human emotions, spirituality, and events. Lewis used the term to describe the cyclical nature of human life and how individuals experience periods of emotional high points and lows, spiritual fervor, and dryness. Like the Buddha's impermanence, 'undulation' is simply another term for the same concept and a central part of the human experience.

However, Lewis took it a step further; he believed it was the difficult times, not the good times, that God used most to draw individuals into relationships. Lewis advanced the idea that God uses the "trough" periods of spiritual dryness not as a punishment but as a tool for spiritual growth. These periods help individuals understand that faith should not be based solely on feelings and the events of the day, which are fleeting and changeable, but rather on a steadfast connection to an unchanging God.

Like wildfires and new beginnings in the desert, this law reflects the idea that our spiritual journey is not a straight, upward path but a series of peaks and troughs, highs and lows. These are all part of our growth and maturation and are designed to move us to become the creatures we were meant to be when we were created.

Once again, meditation is a key practice for cultivating an experiential understanding of impermanence and the "Law of Undulation." Through mindfulness of the breath, sensations, thoughts, and feelings, meditators observe the ceaseless change happening within their own body and mind and deeply appreciate the preciousness and fleeting nature of human life and that they are right where they need to be.

**Josh's Choice**

At this point in the book, I'd like to introduce you to one of my life's heroes, my son Josh. His journey has been one of staggering loss, anguish, and grief—a true "wildfire to new beginnings"—that he has navigated with tremendous courage and resilience. Emerging from the other side, Josh has found tranquility, peace, and a powerful sense of purpose.

As a father, there's nothing more heart-wrenching than witnessing one of your children endure such profound devastation and loss. All I wanted to do was to scoop up my 190 lb. son, cradle him in my arms, and somehow make everything better. Yet, I found myself utterly helpless in the face of his pain, and I believe that was the most challenging aspect for me.

Since that shocking wildfire in 2003, Josh has embarked on an introspective, inspirational, and, at times, devastating journey of healing and transformation. I recently challenged him with an immensely difficult question: "Josh," I asked, "if you could change the most painful and defining event of your life, would you?"

Below, you'll find Josh's answer, articulated in his own words.

My initial reaction to dad's question was, "Definitely!" But, after reflecting, I rethought my answer. Why wouldn't I want to avoid the incomprehensible agony of my deepest, darkest hurts and worst nightmares? Especially when I think of how my dreams and expectations were so suddenly ripped away in such a jolting and seemingly cruel way.

Outwardly, I appeared to 'have it all' during my senior year of high school in 2003. I came from an upper-middle-class family with supportive and loving parents. I was popular, had a beautiful girlfriend, and was the star linebacker on the football team.

As my high school football team entered the state playoffs, we were a top-seed in the western division for the state of North Carolina. We cruised through the early rounds to reach the semi-final game on Thanksgiving Friday. The sky was dark and ominous as rain poured throughout the morning. I worried that our big game might be postponed. Early that afternoon, my sweetheart called and invited me to come visit before I reported to the field for game preparation. As I left, I trotted through the rain to my car, not knowing those would be the last steps I would run in my life. Metaphorical lighting was about to strike, sparking a violent fire of destruction on everything I thought mattered to me most.

The most eerie and enduring memory of my life-changing moment is how quickly the crash occurred and my panic the instant before impact. My car hydroplaned as I sped around a curve, and suddenly everything went dark. I had no time to process my transition into a different existence.

Weeks passed before I recovered sufficient lucidity to grasp the severity of my injuries. My initial realization was that I had missed the big game. My teammates won the semi-finals match-up that night, went on to play, and lost in the championship game a week later. I was heartbroken not to be with my teammates for the thrill of winning and the anguish of defeat. Then, that sadness was overshadowed in the face of a far grimmer, unacceptable reality. Doctors and family gathered around me one morning to attempt the unenviable task of telling a 17-year-old boy that his life as he knew it was over. They explained that my back was broken, compressing my spinal cord, which completely paralyzed me from the waist down. The prospects of regaining any feeling or movement were bleak.

It is difficult to go back and relive the emotions of the first six months after my accident. Could I really be paralyzed? I was a strong, athletic young man, but now powerless, living a cruel nightmare. I felt outside of myself watching a horror movie of my life that would not end. I wept and wailed at night, crying to God to save me. I tried to wiggle my toes, but they remained numb and inert. As it became more and more apparent that nothing was going to save me, I wanted to die.

As far as I knew, this was my only life, and it was now ruined. I would never again feel the cold, wet grass, glistening with morning dew, on my feet as I ran freely. I would never again be a sexually complete person, free to connect intimately through the full feeling and oneness that making love to a woman encompasses. I was resigned to the life of a cripple, pitiful and feeble like an injured dog needing to be put down for its own good. I came to believe that if there was a God, It was evil. There was no justifiable good that could reconcile this type of suffering. My anger and resentment led to lashing out at my family and friends, deception, isolation, and, eventually, addiction.

I will never forget the first time I felt the stunning high of snorting a 30mg Oxycodone pill. It gave me instantaneous relief from my otherwise constant back pain and a euphoric ecstasy, like a snug blanket in winter. Now, I could take temporary escapes to a hospitable oblivion. I eventually began the dangerous experiment of mixing street drugs like heroin and fentanyl into my nose. My tolerance grew. Addiction took hold. Soon, I found that injection was the only way to continue reaching the seeming nothingness that I so craved. I began a descent toward an even darker place than after my accident. I entered hell.

There is a saying that goes something like this: *Religion is for those who are afraid to go to Hell, Recovery is for those who have already been to Hell and don't want to go back.*

Hell, for me, was watching my peers move forward, graduate college, and start families and careers. It was stealing from my family and missing important events. It was sleepless nights, sweating and aching, with chills from withdrawal, unable to control my bladder or bowels. It was having a meth dealer point a gun at my head because of the paranoid delusions of his insomnia. It was spending every penny I could get my hands on, buying my drugs, then pouring them down the toilet because I wanted to stop, only to repeat the vicious cycle. It was crossing every line I said I would never cross and enduring the shame of my fallen state. Most of all, it was feeling dead on the inside, haunted by the ghosts of my past, unable to smile or appreciate anything or anyone.

In April 2017, my family was told by a counselor, "prepare to bury your boy because he will likely be dead from fentanyl in a few weeks." They courageously and desperately intervened one last time. They were both terrified, trying to make peace with my impending death, but their love simply would not let them give up. They met me with one last offer—a one-way plane ticket to a long-term treatment center in Minnesota. Honestly, by that point, I was just so exhausted from fighting. Against my hopelessness and in a moment of grace, I surrendered. I said yes. They drove me to Charlotte and put me on an airplane the next morning.

My sobriety date is April 20th, 2017, the first day of a second, perhaps even third, chance at life that I have been so graciously given. Since then, I have not found using any mood- or mind-altering substance necessary. My surrender led to God granting me the unexpected willingness to be vulnerable and ask for sustaining help. This started in treatment, as I shared my anger and fears with addiction counselors and therapists. My surrender continued as I took suggestions, following small steps toward rebuilding my life. Sometimes quickly, sometimes slowly, the broken relationships and hurt I caused to my family and friends have been healed. I simply let go of control, following directions from professionals and the other recovering addicts who came before me. Positive momentum has helped me become an independent and contributing member of society. Most importantly, my experience makes me qualified to counsel and testify to others who have been severely injured or struggle with addiction.

After five years of continuous sobriety and healing in Minnesota, I returned to school to complete my degree. It is so fulfilling to use my brain in this way again and connect with my professors and peers. I entered the University of Arizona. After two semesters of studying Political Science, Law, and Policy, I have a perfect 4.0 GPA. This, my friends, is a true miracle and something I never thought possible. I plan to attend law school upon graduation and use my experience, knowledge, and skills to love others and give hurting people a voice of representation. They so need to be heard.

Living and choosing to move forward with a disability has given me the gifts of patience, resilience, and humility. I have learned that the world will likely never fit itself into my schedule or expectations. I can choose wisely now in how I push others towards my ends or let go with gratitude. Health challenges beyond my control are always possible, but I have learned not to dwell on them more than necessary and to keep a self-care routine. Finally, I have grown to understand that humility is knowing that "but for the grace of God, there go I," and that I need not think less of myself, but rather, I should try to think of myself less.

This brings me back to dad's big question. If I could change everything and prevent my injury and addiction, would I? My honest answer is—that I am increasingly leaning towards no. That may not sound very satisfying, but it is the truth. My recovery has drastically changed my answer in recent years, even since early sobriety. There is more peace and acceptance now as I seek to *find another way* through sharing the CAST Process and meditations with dad.

One thing I know for sure. The destructive and unforgiving fire that burned down my previous expectations has given me a new, more creative, diverse, and beautiful way of life that I would not change. My recovery has transformed pain into meaning and purpose. My injury and addiction have given me an irreplaceable perspective. My character assets of non-judgment and humility directly result from my pain. I have learned to invest in relationships and community and root myself in something greater than my material circumstances. There is depth and clarity in my goals and purpose. I have learned to love myself and my imperfections and strive for progress over perfection. I finally feel comfortable within myself. Most of all, I feel peace in the fact that my story can reach others with a message of hope and perseverance. If I die tomorrow, there will be peace in my heart, knowing that I have faced my fears and fought the good fight. So, this is my story of an incredibly destructive wildfire and the glorious new beginning that arose from it.

This is Ski; I am back. "*Thank you, Josh! You made your daddy cry again. I am so very proud of you!*"

# Chapter 8 -

# Letting Go

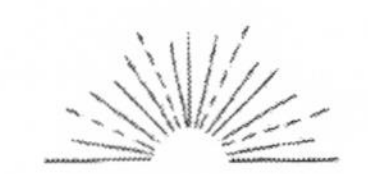

*She let go.*

*Without a thought or a word, she let go.*

*She let go of fear. She let go of the judgments.*
*She let go of the confluence of opinions swarming around her head.*
*She let go of the committee of indecision within her.*
*She let go of all the 'right' reasons. Wholly and completely,*
*without hesitation or worry, she just let go.*

*She didn't ask anyone for advice. She didn't read a*
*book on how to let go... She didn't search the scriptures.*

*She just let go.*
*She let go of all of the memories that held her back.*
*She let go of all of the anxiety that kept her from moving forward.*
*She let go of the planning and all of the calculations about how to do it*
*just right.*

*She didn't promise to let go.*
*She didn't journal about it.*
*She didn't write the projected date in her day-timer.*

*She made no public announcement and put no ad in the paper.*
*She didn't check the weather report or read her daily horoscope.*

*She just let go.*
*She didn't analyze whether she should let go.*
*She didn't call her friends to discuss the matter.*
*She didn't do a five-step Spiritual Mind Treatment.*
*She didn't call the prayer line.*
*She didn't utter one word. She just let go.*

*No one was around when it happened.*
*There was no applause or congratulations.*
*No one thanked her or praised her.*
*No one noticed a thing.*

*Like a leaf falling from a tree, she just let go.*
*There was no effort. There was no struggle.*
*It wasn't good and it wasn't bad.*
*It was what it was, and it is just that.*
*In the space of letting go, she let it all be.*
*A small smile came over her face.*
*A light breeze blew through her.*
*And the sun and the moon shone forevermore.*

— Reverend Safire Rose

This poem by Reverend Safire Rose is truly magnificent. It conveys, perhaps in some of the most profound words I have ever read, the essence of releasing it all and surrendering to what we know as life.

This poem offers three incredibly powerful lessons. The first highlights the beauty and simplicity of letting go. On this particular day, for reasons we may never know, her act of letting go was effortless. The grace and simplicity of this action resonate throughout the poem.

Without a single consideration or utterance, she just did it. She didn't ask for guidance from others, nor did she flip open a book to study how to let go. She didn't pore over sacred texts. She didn't take a vow to help her release her grip. She didn't record her thoughts on paper. She didn't meticulously mark a calendar date for her 'letting go' event. No public declaration was made, no advertisement was placed, and no one was consulted. She didn't consider the reasons why she should let go. No friend was called for a thoughtful discussion about her decision. She didn't reach out to a prayer hotline. Not a single word was spoken. It just happened.

*"She just let go."* Such simplicity, naturalness, and power!

The second transcendent lesson from the poem is centered around what she let go of. Lines like, "She let go of fear... of the judgments... of the confluence of opinions... of all the 'right' reasons... of all of the memories that held her back... of all of the anxiety..." encapsulate her process of giving up all the aspects of her life which burdened her.

Finally, the liberation and relief from letting go shine through her words towards the end of the poem.

"Like a leaf falling from a tree, she just let go. There was no effort…In the space of letting go, she let it all be. A small smile came over her face. A light breeze blew through her. And the sun and the moon shone forevermore."

Her words are a beacon, a lighthouse calling us home from life's painful and destructive storms; They offer an incredibly deep sense of solace.

Reverend Safire Rose, I may not know you personally, but if you read this, let me tell you firsthand that, "I want to be part of your congregation one day." There is such profound freedom in your words.

**Giving Up the Fight**

Surrender is a concept that rubs most Westerners the wrong way. We associate it with defeat, giving up, and hoisting the white flag. This notion defies everything we've been taught since our youth. Take me, for instance, a sports enthusiast and a particularly passionate football fan, coaching both of my sons through their childhood years.

As I pen these words, the thought that sends chills down my spine is the potential unveiling of a hidden recorded version of one of my impassioned halftime speeches to my boys' football teams. What would we hear? We would hear *Me* raising my voice, pressing these young boys to dig deeper, try harder, make their parents and community proud, and become men. Ultimately, I would end this tirade with, "Let's kick some ass, boys!" You see, I was a college athlete, and the idea of surrender was absolutely unthinkable, even in my 40s.

And now, as I write this mindfulness book, I'm asking you to give up the fight, to surrender? What changed me?

A lot. If life is doing its job, we are evolving, we change. In his insightful book, *The Middle Passage*[16], James Hollis explores the concept of a midlife transition as a period where individuals reassess their lives and seek deeper meaning. A key message is that this transition doesn't have to be a crisis, but it can be a reevaluation and awakening process. During this period, we are passaging from the first half of life, largely governed by societal expectations and unconscious conditioning, and climbing (often over others) the corporate ladder towards a more authentic and fulfilling second half of life. I, like Hollis, believe this journey, while very challenging, is a vital part of personal growth and self-realization, allowing us to live more conscious and meaningful lives. This is all to say that I experienced this 'the middle passage' and it profoundly changed me from that ranting, out-of-control football coach to what you are reading today.

Let's get back to the process of letting go with two important questions. First, what are we to surrender to or let go of? Second, how does this act of raising the white flag contribute to our happiness?

**Those 'Damned' Attachments**

What are we letting go of? The one most important answer: *attachments*. These are attachments to our roles, possessions, compulsive need to be right, relationships, and even our very lives. The previous sentence is likely to halt you in your tracks. It held me captive during most of my middle passage, but eventually, I was beaten into submission. It would not be possible for me to find happiness without relinquishing my attachments. There was no alternative. The art of surrender is a narrow gate we must pass through to find serenity, tranquility, fulfilling relationships, and genuine happiness.

Again, I want to come back to something I said at the beginning of the book. Happiness resides in all of us, in our *I*, and we simply have to clear the attachments out of our *Me* to find it. It's just that our unconscious minds are persistently generating unhappiness. It's as simple as that. Take away this self-inflicted unhappiness; what you have left is a happiness that has always been there, waiting to be revealed all along.

What is an attachment? It's an emotional state characterized by clinging. It is driven by the belief that your happiness depends on a particular thing or person. What makes attachments so insidious is they have two sides to them – on one side, you experience a burst of pleasure and thrill when you obtain what you're attached to. However, on the flip side, there is an ever-present sense of threat and tension, a fear of losing the very thing or person that initially brought you that pleasure.

In Buddhist philosophy, suffering is described and dissected in foundational tenets outlined in the "The Four Noble Truths." These principles state that: 1) life always involves suffering in obvious and subtle forms; 2) the root of all suffering is our cravings, our clinging. To put it another way, it is our attachments; 3) to halt suffering, we must *cease our cravings by giving them up, by surrendering our attachments*; and 4) by living ethically, practicing meditation, and developing wisdom, we will gain enlightenment (the eightfold path).

The first three principles are a real paradigm shift for most of us in Western cultures. They essentially say we cannot change the fact that suffering will happen. Despite this fact, our suffering centers around our desire to hold on to things or for things to be different than they are. Then, like a perfect mathematical equation, the Third Noble Truth states that if we want to alleviate our suffering, we must stop craving our attachments to situations, things, people, or having different lives.

There are a few books that are so important to me that I try to read them every year. One such book is psychologist Victor Frankl's *Man's Search for Meaning*[17]. During World War II, Victor Frankl was a prisoner in four Nazi concentration camps, including Auschwitz, and lost his wife, mother, and brother in the Holocaust. Under the worst imaginable circumstances, he wrote, "When we are no longer able to change a situation…we are challenged to change ourselves."

These words leave me profoundly humbled and inspired. Here was a man, defenseless, engulfed in unimaginable cruelty and suffering, and daily, hourly faced with death. Yet, amidst all of this, he found a way to raise himself up, to evolve and change. Each day that we remain captured by our desires and attachments, we give up our chance for genuine freedom and true happiness.

I believe the tragic irony of ironies regarding attachments is that if the things we desire are not fulfilled, we are unhappy. But even if a given desire is achieved, it doesn't bring lasting happiness. It typically is just a fleeting thrill followed by a sense of weariness, followed by the fear of losing the prized possession that has just been obtained. How do we continually fall for this?

You might be wondering by this point in the chapter if we can keep any attachments. Yes, we can keep as many as we want, but with each one, we risk it destroying our happiness. Remember that even if ninety-nine of our attachments are fulfilled in a day, one single unsatisfied attachment typically drives us crazy, eating away our happiness. Is it any wonder that attachments have such power to make us unhappy?

As discussed throughout this book, attachments are deeply ingrained in our evolutionary programming. The only way to win our attachment battle is to surrender them, to let them go. As Safire Rose's beautiful poem illustrates, letting go of attachments is possible.

I believe two fundamental understandings are required to let go. First, we must acknowledge that we are holding on to the false belief that without a particular person or thing, we can't be happy. This requires us to evaluate our beliefs, roles, possessions, and relationships and evaluate them one by one to see the irrationality of holding on to what we cannot control. When we challenge these false beliefs, we will find that attachments will begin to lose their power and grip on us.

The second understanding, and quite frankly, relief, is that we can enjoy things and people without being attached to them. By refusing to cling to the false belief that we can't be happy without them, we're freed from the emotional strain of holding on to them too tight. We can love and appreciate them even more if we don't fear losing them.

Attachments will fall away in the radiant and healthy light of these understandings. However, our light of awareness must shine continuously on them, given their powerful, evolutionarily driven nature. It is vital to remember that attachments can only thrive in the dark illusions of our unconscious minds.

We can do this! We can indeed achieve this transformation. By confronting the roots of our unhappiness fearlessly and fostering awareness through mindfulness, we can gently release our attachments during quiet periods and meditation, as described in Part 2 of the book. As a result, happiness and peace will rise from within, emerging from our core and from our *I*.

**Waiting for Life's Wave**

I recently had a wonderful conversation with my dear friend Glenn. Glenn is the senior pastor of the church I attend and an avid surfer. In contrast to Glenn, I'm an East Coast boy with a love for the surf but little skill to show for it. Glenn was curious about my approach to surfing, and particularly about catching a wave.

I explained how I would paddle out and continuously seek the perfect wave. Spotting a potential wave 20 yards away, I would paddle frantically to reach it, only to invariably miss it. This relentless chase exhausted me as I zigzagged across the water, always seemingly out of sync with the waves. After an hour of little success, I typically would reluctantly head towards the shore, catching a few small wave washes on my way back to my beach towel.

Glenn's response left a lasting impression, a powerful metaphor not just for surfing but for life itself. He beautifully described surfing as a dance with the ocean, a mesmerizing journey on its mystical waves toward the shore. He emphasized that this was not merely about balance and physical prowess; it was also about understanding the ocean's language and interpreting the whispers of its waves.

Surfing was all about waiting, Glenn said. You observe the ocean's rhythm, anticipate a good wave, and then just trust that it will appear at the right time. Once you spot your wave, your dance partner, if you will, then you match its pace and allow it to catch you. The power and speed as the wave lifts you, carries you, "it's exhilarating!" he said. He told me wipeouts were inevitable, but they were also part of the dance.

Glenn pointed out that the heart of my problem was my relentless pursuit of the perfect wave. He contended that if the wave was indeed a dance partner, it wouldn't appreciate me rushing up and demanding a dance. Just like a human dance party, such an aggressive approach would be very unappealing.

He reiterated the importance of understanding the sea's language and respecting its rhythm and boundaries. He emphasized the value of patience and how the right wave would come when I least expected it. When I asked what if it doesn't, he replied, "Sometimes, the ocean knows this just isn't your day to surf. You can trust the ocean. You really can!"

Glenn's parting words struck me deeply. At the end of a surfing day, he said, he would sit on his truck's tailgate, gaze at the ocean, and marvel at the unending waves. They had been doing this for billions of years, and he was sure they would continue forever.

This conversation powerfully illuminated the beautiful analogy between surfing and life. With some sadness, I thought of how much of my life I'd spent paddling vigorously, exhausting myself trying to catch life's beauty when it surrounded me all along. All I had to do was give up the fight, surrender, and get out of life's way, and it would magically appear.

I now realize that only by letting go of expectations, attachments, and control can life provide the most thrilling ride imaginable. When we stop striving for happiness and realize it has always been in us, in our *I* all along, we gain great trust that its magnificence will continue, not only in this lifetime but in all our lifetimes to come.

# Step 4 -

# Trust the Journey

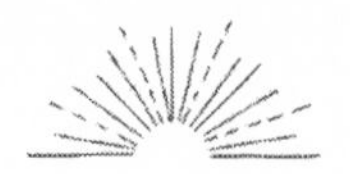

The final two chapters are designed to help us continue to venture beyond the confines of our current perception, our individual sense of self, and into the realization that something infinitely greater exists within and around us. We then begin to sense and trust that this realm of deeper consciousness is not a mythical concept. Rather, it's our deepest human connection to the Creative Intelligence that created the universe and us. Perhaps most surprising is that through stillness, we mere mortals can tap into and become co-creators with the Purposeful Designer of it all.

As we journey further into these waters, we will broaden our comprehension that the keys to freedom and happiness reside in continually loosening our grip on control. We are now on a beautiful sailboat on the open seas. We have unfurled our sails and surrendered to the powerful winds that carry us forward, knowing that this boat is being steered to an enchanted new world, to exactly where we need to be, precisely when we need to be there. By relinquishing the need to control the events of our lives, we open the door to a faith that fosters confidence that everything that unfolds in our lives serves a greater purpose.

In these chapters, I will invite you to spend more time in nature. Breathe it in, learn from it, and allow its innate beauty and intricate design to speak directly to your soul. Marvel at its stillness, a silent testimony to the harmony that exists when we simply let things be and experience them.

In stillness, we will courageously consider our lives on Earth, the brevity of it, the certainty of death. Here, I will ask us to step back from much of what we've been taught about God and religion and peel away layers of dogma and doctrine that may have inadvertently harmed us. You see, as extraordinary as they are, our minds are bound by limitations. The Divine, however, is not. By surrendering our restrictive ideas and accepting our inability to fully comprehend the infinite, we create space for a direct, unfiltered experience of the Divine.

The last leg of this journey is a return to simplicity. It's about becoming a child again. We can't use logic and empiricism to solve life's most profound riddles. We can't dissect the Divine or decode the mystery of existence post-death into a series of rational equations. These waters are too deep for rational thought; thus, they invite us instead to simply experience, to surrender to the mystery, beauty, and miracle of it all.

By letting go of our desperate need to know and embracing the unknowables, we will unlock our capacity to live powerfully and fearlessly. *We will feel so alive!* This is ultimate freedom, an existence filled with happiness that isn't conditional but arises from deep within. So, let us all sail together on this last leg of our journey as we gain an unending trust in the magic that is our unique path and explore the infinite potential within and around us.

# Chapter 9 -

# My Path from Science to the Sacred

### I Pooped in Mama's Potatoes

My fifty-plus-year love affair with science actually started at age eight when I stood behind my family's tobacco barn and looked into the heavens through a primitive telescope my parents had saved for. Fast forward a decade. I vividly remember my first trip home during my sophomore year at Western Carolina University. It was a five-hour trip through the mountains to my home in Pilot Mountain, North Carolina. After a year of partying, participating on the college track team, and finishing with a 1.6 GPA, I decided it was time to get serious and became a biology major. Back in those days, we could not come home from college often and spoke to our parents, at most, once a week from a pay phone in the middle of the dorm. I had been in school for about two months and, for the first time, was particularly excited about a class called "Genetics and Evolution." In fact, I was even doing really well in a class for the first time. I had not told my parents that I was taking this course. I particularly had not told my dad, given his view on the topic of evolution and the fact that we attended a Southern Baptist Church, where this type of academic activity would've been highly frowned upon.

My parents were so excited about having me home that they decided to invite the families of several of our closest friends. My mom had fixed all my favorites: chicken and dumplings, mashed potatoes with "sawmill" gravy, black-eyed peas, and black heart cherry cobbler. Dad sat at the head of the table, grinning with a Marlboro dangling from the corner of his mouth. The first hour of this party went incredibly well. But then, for reasons I still don't understand, I decided it was time to give this celebratory gathering a lesson on all the new things that I'd learned in college, especially from the class I enjoyed the most, the 'evolution class.'

I'm not certain I could have caused a more uncomfortable moment if I had stood on the kitchen table and pooped in mom's mashed potatoes. I was so excited to explain Darwin's principle of natural selection and how single-cell organisms arose about 400 million years ago, followed by plants and then animals crawling out of the water, eventually giving rise to dinosaurs and mammals, including us. I remember my dad looking at me and saying, "If this is what they're teaching you at that fancy college, you might as well come back home!"

We were both stubborn and so the argument that followed raged on for hours while our guests left in pure exasperation and exhaustion. I don't want to leave you with a bad impression of my father because he was my hero, and we actually published a scientific paper together before he died. He was just not ready, and I was just not educated enough to have this discussion. I remember his last words to me at the party, and they were true, "You think you are so smart, but you are just smart enough to be very dangerous!"

**Science and Religion's Nasty Relationship**

The argument between my dad and me was a small example of the larger debate occurring in the 1970s that is still alive today. Science and religion have had a nasty, antagonistic relationship for centuries. From the introduction of Galileo's hypotheses that the earth circled the sun, through Darwin's explanation of the theory of natural selection and evolution, science and religion, and particularly scientific materialism and extreme biblical literalism, have been at war.

As we get into the "Trust the Journey" section of this book, I want to address a fundamental confusion I believe persists with the term God. Framed largely by Western models, "God" is referred to by the pronoun "he" as a father figure, but more problematically, a fearsome, vindictive father that invokes unworthiness and misery for many Western seekers. For these and other reasons, "God" has been a difficult term to use in interreligious, spiritual, and religion-science dialogues. But I don't want preconceptions about God to impede readers of this book as I have already used it several times. Thomas Keating, in his book *Reflections on the Unknowable*[18], says that perhaps the best description of God is 'is-ness' without any limit, 'I am,' without any other pronoun. I affirm Keating's broader way of thinking about God. You may have noticed I have already used terms such as "the Divine," several times in this book. I also am very comfortable with terms such as "Creative Intelligence," "Purposeful Designer," "the Beloved," and "God." These resonant for me with Keating's limitless 'is-ness'.

In 1999, eminent paleontologist, evolutionary biologist, and historian of science, Stephen Jay Gould, pointed out in his book, *Rocks of Ages*[19], that the science-religion debate is largely unnecessary. Science and religion, Gould explains, explore separate domains, ask very different questions, and utilize vastly dissimilar tools to answer them. Consequently, there can and should be no debate between science and religion because there is no overlap between their areas of study and types of expertise.

Gould called this the principle of "Non-Overlapping Magisteria." He suggests this principle "enjoys strong and fully explicit support, even from the primary cultural stereotypes of hard-line traditionalism" and is "a sound position of general consensus, established by long struggle among people of goodwill." I could not agree more. I have dear friends in both the religious literalism and scientific materialism camps that have participated in these unnecessary debates, harming others in the process, and I respectfully believe it's time to move forward and leave these old arguments behind.

**Scientific Facts and Mysteries**

In this chapter, I will point out indisputable scientific truths and, at the same time, call attention to mysteries where even the most rational, objective individual may consider a Designer who placed intelligence in the universe from its beginning. Let me start with a disclaimer. It is not possible to provide a detailed examination of the intersection of science and faith in one short chapter. My objective is to describe my journey that led to a beautiful harmony between my day job as a scientist and my spiritual awareness of a Divine creator. For a more in-depth discussion of this fascinating topic, two of my favorite books are *The Language of God*[20], by one of the world's leading scientists and former director of the Human Genome Project and the National Institutes of Health, Dr. Francis Collins, and *God According to God*[21], by MIT-trained physicist and theologian Gerald Schroeder.

I will start with what has been called the super-ultimate question. Why is there existence in the first place, and why do you and I exist? Perhaps even more astonishing than our existence is the fact that our existence includes our incredible minds capable of wondering why the whole thing, including us, exists. This riddle is unsolvable. While it is possible to conceive that nothing should exist, you would need to exist to imagine it. But the fact is that we do exist, and there is overwhelming scientific evidence that our existence, along with time and matter, began with a massive explosion of energy known as The Big Bang. As you will see in the next chapter, the fact of our existence now is such a miracle that I find the idea of existing after death in some form is not implausible at all, but quite likely.

There is now a consensus among scientists that 14 billion years ago, the universe emerged in a single instant from a massive explosion of an infinitely dense point of pure energy. Energy rapidly transitioned to matter (as was shown possible by Albert Einstein's famous equation,

$e=mc^2$). These events theoretically should have created equal quantities of matter and anti-matter. That is a big deal because matter and anti-matter are oppositely charged, and if they come in contact, they annihilate each other to go back to pure energy.

All life forms, the Earth, and stellar objects are matter. That this is the case presents us with an unexplained asymmetry in our universe, which slightly favors matter over anti-matter. Why asymmetry, and how did that come about?

And then there is the precision, often referred to as our 'fine-tuned universe.' Hundreds of conditions and scientific constants appear to have been tuned in an extraordinarily precise and unpredicted way in order to make the formation of the universe and the emergence of life possible. These values had to be in place and could not have been even slightly different and still given rise to our expanding universe with all of it marvelous complexities, a life-giving planet Earth, or the reality of me sitting here at this moment writing this book. Francis Collins explains this unpredictable fine-tuning:

"Altogether, there are fifteen physical constants whose values current theory is unable to predict. They are givens: they simply have the value that they have. This list includes the speed of light, the strength of the weak and strong nuclear forces, various parameters associated with electromagnetism, and the force of gravity. The chance that all of these constants would take on the values necessary to result in a stable universe capable of sustaining complex life forms is almost infinitesimal. And yet those are exactly the parameters that we observe. In sum, our universe is wildly improbable."[20]

So, the "wildly improbable" nature of the universe places scientists, non-scientists, religious, and New Age practitioners on the same footing regarding the reason(s) behind our existence. For theists, the Big Bang and fine-tuned universe has been compared to a Creative Designer that has simultaneously tuned a large number of dials to an incredibly narrow range to render our universe and life possible. Even atheists or agonistics view these conditions and constants with awe. Sir Fred Hoyle, the astronomer responsible for the theory of nucleosynthesis, wrote, "A commonsense interpretation of the facts suggests that a super-intellect has monkeyed with physics, as well as with chemistry and biology." Even Stephen Hawkins, in his classic *A Brief History of Time*[22], noted that "The remarkable fact is that the values of these numbers seem to have been very finely adjusted to make possible the development of life."

However, to be fair, many scientists argue that theories such as multiverse universes replace the need for a Designer. According to this theory, the multiverse is a group of hypothetical universes (parallel or alternative), each with their own unique physical laws and constants, and the only reason we regard ours as so 'fine-tuned' is that it is the only one that we have access to. In other words, only universes that were hospitable to the evolution of beings such as us would be capable of considering the issue of a fine-tuned universe. However, this again brings us all back to the super-ultimate question of why existence at all, whether it be one universe or billions.

After the Big Bang, the universe continued to expand for the next million or so years. Then, the gravitational force began to bring together spiraling galaxies as stars formed, including our own sun approximately 5 billion years ago. Our earth formed about 4 billion years ago, and within the first 200 million years after its formation, the earth was filled with replicating microbial life. Okay, I have to stop here again.

As a card-carrying scientist with a Ph.D. in biochemist, I have an absolute love and reverence for all the coordinated cellular and molecular events necessary for life's development. I am left in complete awe when I consider that life developed from inanimate matter at all, but especially in such a relatively short amount of time. Famous scientific experiments have been performed to try to replicate the conditions of that time by sending an electrical charge representing lightning into a flask containing basic elements. These have shown that a few organic compounds, including amino acids can be formed. However, this simple experiment pales in comparison to what really happened, the formation of complex, self-replicating microbes with multifaceted molecules and structures such as RNA, proteins, and membranes.

Not only did these microbes reproduce, but they contained genetic information and variation that allowed them to evolve in complexity, giving rise to organisms like cyanobacteria, which utilized water and light during photosynthesis to produce oxygen as a byproduct. Over time, cyanobacteria released enough oxygen into Earth's atmosphere that it was possible for creatures like us to evolve to use that very same oxygen for respiration. *It seems as if the universe 'knew' we were coming.* The purposeful nature of this almost unfathomable progression and particularly the awe-inspiring structure of DNA is beautifully stated by Gerald Schroder, "Identical reproduction, a copying machine, yields stasis. What was needed and what nature produced was a molecule that could reproduce and change, somehow borrowing resources from its immediate environment until it became a cell. But reproduction is purpose-driven, the continuation of the line. That prebiotic molecule, whether by design or by dumb luck, had purpose within it from its inception."[21]

It would be another 3.5 billion years until diverse invertebrates arose, bringing about what has been called the "Cambrian explosion", and then plants appeared on dry land about 400 million years ago. Dinosaurs ruled the earth, beginning about 230 million years ago. They suddenly disappeared at a time period when a large asteroid hit the Yucatan peninsula, leading to catastrophic climate change and the subsequent rise of mammals. The first human ancestors walking on two legs appeared 5.8 million years ago, followed by numerous hominid species over the next 5.5 million years. The first record of modern humans (*Homo sapiens*) appeared about 195,000 years ago in Africa, and they (we) migrated into Europe and Asia less than 100,000 years ago and eventually into the Americas around 30,000 years ago.

**Nature's Crowing Achievement**

The crowning achievement of evolution was its virtuoso design of the human brain with its 100 billion neurons, 10 trillion nerve interconnections, and an estimated storage capacity of $1.25 \times 10^{12}$ bytes.

Brain shape and complexity comparable to present-day humans occurred ~80,00 years ago. Archeological evidence, especially around the burial sites of these populations, began to show signs of abstract reasoning and the capacity to differentiate themselves as individuals. These social changes were mirrored by radical advances in technology, the development of economies, and the great geographic expansion of populations. It was also about this time that these early humans also began to display proof that they were capable of deep love and relationships. For instance, they mourned the death of their loved ones by placing their most valuable possessions in the gravesites of the deceased.

Concisely stated, this journey started with the burst of energy (from nothing) of The Big Bang that then became a matter that somehow gave rise to life. But not just any life, it was life with a mind that somehow knows, questions, creates, and is capable of conscious awareness. While science has discovered a great deal about the characteristics of the brain, including its morphology and communication networks, no one understands the mysterious inner world of consciousness. The late Harvard University Nobel laureate, George Wald, stated in his essay "Life and Mind in the Universe," "It is mind that has composed a physical universe that breeds life and, so eventually evolves creatures that know and create: science-, art-, and technology- making animals. In them, the universe begins to know itself."

At the center of this rapid tour of life's emergence is a process known as evolution, the observation that diverse groups of microbes, plants, and animals (including humans) descended from a small set of common ancestors. In 1859, Charles Darwin published *The Origin of Species*[23], which proposed that natural selection and the resulting adaptations represent the primary mechanism that drives life's increasing complexity. This theory was based largely on his observations of diverse life forms in South America, particularly the Galapagos Islands, and the theory was shared by Alfred Russell Wallace, who independently came to the same conclusion. Darwin also recognized his theory applied to humans and wrote a second book, *The Descent of Man*[24]. Darwin concluded *The Origin of the Species*[23] with "There is grandeur in this view of life, with its several powers, having been originally breathed by the Creator into a few forms or into one..." Despite these words acknowledging a Creator, Darwin had metaphorically "stood up on the kitchen table and pooped in religion's mashed potatoes." Literalist groups of all religious faiths continue to argue for a Creator who designed all plants and animals individually in a very limited span of time (e.g. 6000 yrs.).

Let me be very clear. For biologists, including medical scientists such as myself, and as stated in Theodosius Dobzhansky's 1973 essay, "Nothing in Biology Makes Sense Except in the Light of Evolution." Evolution is the basis of all biological and medical work, and no serious scientist doubts it as the foundation for studying the beautiful complexity and diversity of life. Dobzhansky also espoused the theistic evolution perspective in which evolution is Divine and provides a means by which nature was created and improved upon throughout time.

**A Universe with a Purpose**

Much of the work of my day job is founded on the science of evolution and genetics. Like Dobzhansky, this knowledge has only enhanced the spiritual awe I find in my work. I study how genetic variation initially developed in humans in Africa and then continued as humans migrated out of Africa and across the globe over the past 100,000 years. Natural selection did its job each time humans were exposed to potentially devastating changes, such as new climates, UV light, pathogens, and restricted food sources. This resulted in a variety of uniquely adapted early populations in different regions of the world. This understanding is vital to our work as we attempt to understand why certain populations in the US and around the globe are more negatively impacted than others by modern Western diets and lifestyles, which result in diseases such as cancer, heart disease, and Alzheimer's disease. With evolution as an underpinning, our overall objective is to personalize diets, lifestyles, and health based on genetics to optimize well-being. This area of research is referred to as precision health and precision medicine and represents a rapidly emerging revolution in healthcare.

As I ponder the history of the monumental scientific discoveries, and especially those that describe the perfection of nature's laws for sustaining life and enhancing diversity and complexity, I see a universe with a purpose, an intelligence within, and this creative force has been present from the very beginning. I stand with the Psalmist as he affirms, "The heavens declare the glory of God; the skies proclaim the work of his hands" (Psalm 19:1). However, the reader doesn't need to share my beliefs to benefit from this book. A critical part of my meditative journey has been to let go of and be liberated from dogmas and perhaps more importantly, my need to defend them.

So, through exploring science's truths and mysteries, I have chosen to believe and *trust* in a Purposeful Designer of the universe. I love the quote by Robert Jastrow (1925-2008), the American astronomer, planetary physicist, and a popular science writer. In his 1978 book, *God and the Astronomers*[25], he explored the intersection of science and religion. As a professed agnostic, he wrote these compelling words, "At this moment, it seems as though science will never be able to raise the curtain on the mystery of creation. For the scientist who has lived by his faith in the power of reason, the story ends like a bad dream. He has scaled the mountains of ignorance; he is about to conquer the highest peak; as he pulls himself over the final rock, he is greeted by a band of theologians who have been sitting there for centuries."

# Chapter 10 -

# Embracing the Unknowables

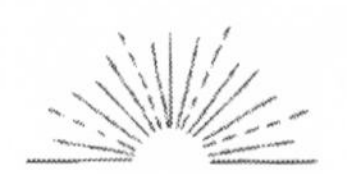

## Lessons from the Bottom of the Grand Canyon

As I touched upon in Chapter 6, although we subconsciously comprehend that our time on Earth is finite, this crucial reality often remains a mere theoretical concept until the prospect of our death, or that of a loved one, looms before us for the first time. Three summers ago, my wife and I had the once-in-a-lifetime experience of spending two weeks rafting the Colorado River at the base of the Grand Canyon. As you've learned, most of my greatest adventures seem to come with powerful life lessons, and my experience at the bottom of the Grand Canyon was not to disappoint.

The first lesson was a realization of my smallness and seeming insignificance at the Canyon's base. Looking up in awe at the towering 3,000-foot walls, I was struck by their geological timeline, from the vivid red and white limestone at the top to the 1.8-billion-year-old Vishnu basement rocks at the bottom. Exposed was nearly 2 billion (yes, billion with a "b") years of geological and biological history. This grand testament to the Earth's lifespan stood as a stark reminder of the fleeting brevity of my existence and, indeed, of all human life in its present form.

Being the scientific nerd that you already know that I am, I did the calculation, and my 80-to-100-year life span was 1/50 billion$^{th}$ of the time revealed in those walls, a tiny drop in an ocean of time. It seemed so meaningless and insignificant; I kept asking, "what in the hell is this all about?" And yet, this is my time here on Earth. It is all I know. So, it and how it ends or begins again means everything to me.

In *The Rewired Brain*[5], I compared our life's journey to a river where we emerge from our mother's womb to become part of this grand river adventure. I emphasized, as I have throughout this book, how important it was to not allow fear arising largely from our unconscious *Me* to cause us to resist the flow of the river, nor to put down our feet to slow us, nor to pick up heavy rocks (such anxieties arising from our past or worries about the future) along the way. Each prevents us from completing the adventure that was individually and intentionally designed for us. We are to simply accept and revel in our journey/adventure, realizing that all of it is a miracle, and have great faith that the river is carrying us to where we were meant to be. But maintaining our joy and peace can be incredibly challenging when we are forced to consider our own mortality or the mortality of someone we deeply love. Knowing life's brevity and sensing all the unknowables that we have no control over when our life ends can be, as Erich Fromm said, "an unbearable prison."

Ram Dass, in his book, *Still Here*[26], beautifully adds his version of a river metaphor that includes facing death. He writes that facing a death, due either naturally or to a potentially lethal diagnosis, is like a bend in that river. Only this time, we can't see around the bend. And before we travel around it, we often endure some rough rapids in the form of painful and devastating changes to our physical and emotional health. I strongly believe that preparing for the rapids before we reach them is vital. If we don't, we are often badly beaten up by what is to come. But, if we prepare, we will have the capacity to take what could become the most important and invigorating ride of our lives.

As you have already learned from this book, I have had the opportunity to confront a cancer diagnosis on three separate occasions, giving me experience in facing these potentially terrifying rapids. My reactions and responses changed dramatically from my first diagnosis to my most recent. The first was, understandably, the reactive response of a complete freak out and ensuing meltdown. The most recent diagnosis was much more mindful, consisting of a deep knowing that there is a benevolent force and Purposeful Designer (described in the previous chapter) within me that will serve as my guide to profound beauty and aliveness if I am willing to accept and surrender to this transcendent adventure.

My cancer diagnoses had also revealed that facing our mortality has incredible power to act as a potent catalyst, propelling us to make vital and often challenging choices that reshape the path of our lives. Were we immortal, nothing at all would hold any significance. It's within these moments of choice that we are compelled to move towards the 'deep end of the pool' where we can unravel the profound meanings of both life and death.

The question you may be asking is, what brought about these changes in perspective? The answer to that question is this; I transitioned from a state of deep fear towards life's unknowable aspects to joyfully embracing life's most profound questions, including the mystery of death. *How?*

**Religious Formulas that No Longer Work**

As you have undoubtedly surmised by now, the writings of C.S. Lewis have profoundly affected how I perceive life. Lewis's body of work spans both fiction and non-fiction, including *The Chronicles of Narnia*[27], *Mere Christianity*[28], and *The Screwtape Letters*[15]. In his poignant book, *A Grief Observed*[29], he details the intense emotional and spiritual storm he weathered following the death of his beloved wife, American poet, Joy Davidman.

This book shook me to the core as my most revered and authoritative hero details how he totally lost his way and his faith after her death. The book was originally published under the pseudonym N.W. Clerk to maintain Lewis's anonymity, and his authorship was not revealed until

1963, the same year he passed away. Subsequent publications of *A Grief Observed*[29] included Lewis's name. I believe Lewis published under a pseudonym to be able to express his raw feelings of grief, pain, and doubt freely and honestly without impacting the faith of those of us who loved him. Truthfully, this book has been a great source of distress and comfort as I have navigated the great unknowables of life.

Lewis's thoughts and emotions are unfiltered throughout the book, bringing us face-to-face with the excruciating truth of his loss. He begins the book in a state of abject disbelief and horror at the loss of his wife. He describes his anguish as a beast inducing fear and a ceaseless sea of crashing waves. He details the mourning for a lost loved one and the shock that seizes his soul in this time of loss.

Perhaps the most alarming and frightening aspect was Lewis's questioning of his own beliefs. His pain and grief lead him to have profound doubts and confusion about his faith, the character of God, and the purpose of pain. He questioned, is God truly good or even present?

One of my all-time favorite movies is, naturally, *Shadowlands*, a 1993 British biographical drama that chronicles the relationship between Lewis (portrayed by Anthony Hopkins) and Davidman (played by Debra Winger). Following Joy's death, Lewis delivers a powerful monologue reflecting on his transformed understanding of God and suffering:

*"God knows, but does God care?*

*We see so little here. We're not the creators.*

*We're the creatures, aren't we?*

*We're the rats in the cosmic laboratory.*

*I have no doubt the experiment is for our own good, but...*

*it still casts God as the vivisectionist, doesn't it?*

*It won't do.*

*It's this bloody awful mess, and that's all there is to it.*

*I'm sorry. I am sorry.*

*I'm simply not fit company tonight."*

This discourse absolutely takes my breath away. My hero, arguably the greatest Christian writer of the 20th century, has completely lost his way and his faith. Many of Lewis's earlier religious formulas now have clearly been placed into doubt.

As *A Grief Observed* draws to a close, Lewis slowly begins to find small pieces of tranquility. He starts to find solace in his memories, and his faith, though shaken to its core, begins to regain a bit of its footing. During the agonizing process depicted in the book, Lewis's view of God evolves from a seemingly cruel and malicious entity to a mysterious presence that defies simple categorizations and definitions.

In my earlier work, *The Rewired Brain*[5], I described an intense period when I was grappling with debilitating shame based on an unfortunate religious formula. You see, the religious doctrine from my childhood in the farmlands of North Carolina greatly emphasized one's 'sins' and demanded a disciplined, hard-working, and morally upright lifestyle. The looming threat was clear—if you failed to live righteously, you and your family would experience God's wrath and ultimately be condemned to eternal hellfire. With this strict and unforgiving framework deeply embedded in my unconscious mind, my conscious self became consumed with guilt, somehow believing that Josh's accident and ensuing paralysis were punishments for my moral shortcomings. It was a cruel period; within a year, I had lost my marriage, company, job, and now, Josh's paralysis. The guilt and shame were unbearable; if my actions had caused Josh's accident, I did not want to live.

On one particularly devastating day, I was making my familiar drive to Atlanta, Georgia to visit Josh at the Shephard Spinal Center. My spirit for life was gone, as I existed in a pure state of desperation. I cried uncontrollably as I raced down the lonely stretches of Carolinas and Georgia highways exceeding 100 miles per hour. My cell phone kept insistently ringing, but I simply ignored it. Finally, I picked it up, shouted, "Leave me the hell alone!" and hung up.

However, the incoming calls persisted. Finally realizing it was my younger sister Tanya, I reluctantly picked up. Despite our love for each other, Tanya and I have been fighting since childhood. Between my gut-wrenching sobs, I listened as she sternly ordered me to pull over. "Don't you understand that you could wreck and kill someone in such a crazy, emotional state?" she said.

Following her instructions, I pulled off to the side of the road, collected my breath, and, in hushed whispers, shared my feelings of overwhelming guilt and shame. I confided in her that if I were to blame for Josh's suffering, I saw no reason to continue living.

Tanya, true to form, was devoid of sympathy but abundant in wisdom. She said, "Would you shut up for a minute?" She paused and then laid into me with a harsh, "You're just a big old fake, aren't you, Ski? You don't believe a damn thing that you have been teaching in Sunday School and church all these years."

"Wait, what do you mean?" I shot back, my mind racing to understand her abruptness and seeming insensitivity.

"Ski, you get a new slate every day. As long as you are sorry and have asked for forgiveness, you have been forgiven, and all is forgotten then," she explained. "You had a clean tab yesterday, the day before, and the day before. So, Josh's accident could not have been your fault. What on earth is wrong with you? You know full well that grace is the centerpiece of our faith. It's the only way any of us can really be free!"

In her rebuke, I found truth. How could I have overlooked the fundamental principle of grace that underpins our faith?

**Unlearning Formulas**

When it comes to God and religion, we often need to unlearn much of what we've been taught. This requires awareness of the illusions we've constructed over a lifetime. For me, this has been a process in which discovering who God is equates to discovering who God is not. Again, it's peeling back the layers, only this time, of my religious formula. I have found that by letting go of many of my destructive religious concepts and humbly understanding that I, my little brain, no matter how complex can never comprehend this, I open myself to a direct, unmediated experience of God.

There's this beautiful piece of wisdom in Eastern spirituality that is known as "pointing at the moon." In this metaphor, the finger is pointing toward the moon. But, and this is key, the finger is *not* the moon. It's merely a guide to direct our gaze towards the ultimate reality, the authentic truth, and the awe-inspiring Divine – 'the moon'.

I imagine the teachings and scriptures we encounter in our spiritual journeys as a finger-pointing to the grand Divine. We also can't get trapped in our religious programming, as I did with my view of Josh's accident and Lewis did with Joy's death. If we hold on to certain incorrect religious formulas, they can destroy us when our lives fall apart.

For me, my Christianity, specifically following Jesus's teachings, serves as an illuminating roadmap, my 'pointing finger' to God. His incredibly mindful teachings are a priceless guide to experience a majestic God. However, as important as teachings and scriptures are, as Anthony de Mellow would often say, "don't mistake the menu for the meal.[30]"

I believe it is also vital not to get turned off to the idea of God by all the false teachings and hypocritical behavior of those who profess belief. As I write this book, somehow Jesus's teachings are being associated with Christian nationalism, politics, gun rights, horrible treatment of immigrants, discrimination against anyone who is different, and the exclusivity of Christianity. I am absolutely horrified.

However, as Francis Collins said in his landmark book, *The Language of God*[20], "keep in mind that the pure water of spiritual truth is carried in those rusty containers called human beings, so there should be no surprise that at times those foundational beliefs can be severely distorted. Do not rest your evaluation of faith, therefore, on what you see in the behavior of individual humans or of organized religion. Rest it instead on the timeless spiritual truths that faith presents."

So, what have been my harmful illusions about God that I believe need to be unlearned? As I mentioned earlier, the God of my upbringing was depicted as an angry, wrathful judge, ever ready to condemn and punish. This image of God breeds fear, guilt, and anxiety, often supporting abusive power structures in religious institutions. This belief often coincides with the notion that God is exclusively 'owned' by a particular religion or belief system and that only literal, often misinterpreted and out-of-context, versions of sacred texts are to be accepted. Collectively, these have the capacity to give rise to highly damaging, authoritarian forms of religion, which have led to the death of millions of people and constant tension and conflict between different religions. For instance, during the Crusades, entire cities were massacred following their capture by invading armies. The hostilities between Christianity and Islam from this period of the Middle Ages are still felt today.

I believe that other harmful illusions include: 1) Viewing God as exclusively male, which can unconsciously reinforce patriarchal structures and undermine the value and role of women; 2) Believing God controls every minute detail of our lives, which can potentially limit human responsibility and accountability; or 3) Perceiving God as a being who exists to fulfill our economic and other desires, which can lead to a transactional faith.

There is much to be unlearned, but as we do, we expand our capacity to experience, co-create, play, and rest in the mystical and sacred space of the Divine. It's not just about unlearning concepts of God; it's about disconnecting us from the empirical need to label and create formulas for everything. It's about learning to accept, enjoy, experience, and embrace unsolvable mysteries and incomprehensible miracles. It's about understanding that we can't describe concepts like truth, God, the 'moon'; we can only point to them.

### Becoming Like a Little Child, Again

For me, embracing the unknowables, including God's nature, has been an "Arizona two step dance." As described above, the initial step involved unlearning preconceived notions about God and recognizing my limited ability to comprehend the mystifying foundations underpinning our lives. The second step may surprise you, but I believe it is becoming like a little child again, with all the curiosity, sense of wonder, boundless imagination, and unabashed joy of a child.

Growing up, we may not have had a lot of money, but there was one tradition that was not to be violated. The Chilton family, typically 20 to 30 of us, would always make a pilgrimage to Myrtle Beach for the week of the 4th of July. These trips and the stories that came out of them remain my most precious memories.

My father was the freest man I ever knew, and I remember that everything was always the "best" to him. He ate the "best" pie, watched the "best" sunset, but when we arrived at the beach, everything escalated to "the best" on steroids. From the moment he laid down the large family blanket, it was 'game on'. A Chilton rule was that no one could enter the ocean without running at full speed toward the waves.

My dad lived fully in the present, so each day at the beach was indeed the best he'd ever had. There was no past to compare it to. He wasn't shackled by yesteryears or tormented by past fears. He was a crazy man, as he reveled only in this present moment at Myrtle Beach, with his family and that old Carolina beach soul R&B shag music. BTW, if you are from England, this music is not what you think.

From the time my sisters and I could walk, our parents would sit us at the ocean's edge, where we would spend hours playing. The beach is an infinite playground of possibilities for children. We were magnetically drawn toward the lapping waves of the ocean. Our tiny feet left fleeting imprints as we sprinted toward the alluring water. Our uncontrollable giggles echoed as we playfully dodged the foamy white breakers. Unexpected waves would catch us off guard and topple us over, triggering ecstatic squeals of delight.

We would then sit down, our little hands sifting through the sand in search of beautiful seashells, curious stones, hidden treasures, or fast-moving crabs washed ashore. Each discovery, regardless of its size or significance, was celebrated as if we had just won an Olympic medal. Our untamed curiosity and sense of wonder seemed to know no limits.

Eventually, we would move a few yards back from the water, our hands, buckets, and small shovels busily engaged in building the most magnificent sandcastles. Our castles featured intricate towers, moats, and bridges. There seemed no end to our boundless imaginations and capacity to innovate. Eventually, the rising tide would reclaim our masterpieces as we sat there with resilient smiles, fully aware that we'd construct an even grander castle the following day.

As we age, what happens to all that beauty, imagination, innocence, and joy we effortlessly embraced as children? Why do we grow up and leave it all behind? I believe it is no accident that many spiritual traditions emphasize returning to a childlike state of being as a path to spiritual enlightenment and connection to the Divine. In my own Christian tradition, Jesus said, "Truly I tell you, unless you change and become like little children, you will never enter the kingdom of heaven." (Matthew 18:3). Similar concepts exist in the Buddhist tradition, which encourages a "beginner's mind" or "Shoshin." In the Hindu Bhagavad Gita, Lord Krishna advises Arjuna to approach spiritual teachings with the innocence and trust of a child, free of ego and preconceived notions.

To know God and joyfully accept life's unknowns, we must change and become like little children again. What does that even mean? It is realizing that life's most profound questions can't be tackled with mere empiricism and logic. When we exhaust pragmatic empiricism, we must wade into the simpler, more mysterious, beautiful waters of experiencing. To experience the Divine and embrace the riddle of our continued existence after the death of our current body, we must become children again.

*We can become children again!* Eckhart Tolle's book *A New Earth: Awakening to Your Life's Purpose*[3] opens with a profound reflection on the role of flowers in human evolution and the significance of our ability to appreciate their beauty. Tolle suggests that the arrival of flowers on earth signified a pivotal moment in the evolution of human consciousness. It was the birth of our ability to appreciate and value beauty for its own sake rather than for survival or utilitarian purposes. This shift involved the capacity to appreciate the 'is-ness' or 'such-ness' of things, to see beauty and value in the mere existence of something, separate from its utility or any need to label it.

That is what a child does. A child observes nature with an unfiltered sense of wonder and curiosity. With an open mind, they explore the world through all their senses, fascinated by every detail, from the movement of a caterpillar to the pattern of a leaf's veins. They engage playfully and directly with everything around them, climbing trees or jumping in puddles. Their observations are personal and intimate, not weighed down by a need to understand or label but filled with a simple appreciation for the beauty around them. This immersive and emotionally engaging approach creates a deep, intuitive connection with the natural world.

So here is my challenge to you. The next time you spot a beautiful flower, walk right up to it like a child and look very closely. Notice its brilliant colors and the perfect symmetry and patterns within the flower; smell its unique and alluring fragrance; sense its energy that is simultaneously so calming and invigorating. This flower, every flower if we allow it, possesses a beauty that will appeal to our senses and emotions and transcend ordinary experiences to connect with something much deeper within us.

Why is this so extremely hard for us in Western cultures? Why do we feel the need to spout off facts to show how smart we are? Instead of naming every tree in the forest or every bird in the sky, we can simply observe them, enjoy their magnificence, and feel their energy. *The next time you walk outside and look up at a magnificent sky full of stars, you will likely feel the need to point out specific stars or constellations, don't!* Just enjoy the wonder of the heavens, marvel at the space between the stars, and the mystery of it all.

You can also do this within your own body. Take a moment to experience your body's miraculous workings that occur every moment without your awareness. Sit and move your focus from one part of your body to another, feeling their sensations without identifying them. Listen for your heartbeat as it tirelessly keeps you alive without any conscious effort from us. Feel the energy coming from your fingertips. *You are a miracle…this all is a miracle!*

Once we can wholeheartedly embrace the breathtaking marvels of life and nature all around us as a child, I am convinced that our capacity to joyously ponder the vast unknowns, including our transcendental nature, will expand dramatically.

# Epilogue -

# A Call to Action

At this juncture in time, I am deeply concerned about the intolerance and lack of love and compassion in our world, particularly in counties like the United States. Like humans, societies experience periods of emotional, spiritual, and event-based ebbs and flows, and presently, I sense a profound low within our society. In my previous work, *The Rewired Brain*[5], I highlighted the dangers of tribalism and how it, coupled with wealth disparities, unconscious fears, ignorance, pride, and anger, can render societies and individuals exceptionally volatile. I fear our society has been drawn into this vortex again over the past six to eight years.

The antidote lies in freedom from fear, prejudice, and intolerance. As discussed throughout this book, we must shift our life's perspective and reorient our minds. It is crucial to understand that my true *Self*, my *I*, is distinct from my body, and my body is merely a vessel that houses this spirit temporarily. No matter what happens to my body, such as illness, aging, decay, and even death, my spirit will endure. As I learned on my first trip to Africa, my transcendent spirit, my *I*, is spiritually linked to others, especially those in need. I instantly discovered that *I* had a hallowed responsibility to provide unconditional love to all inhabitants of this earth. If *I* followed this call, I sensed that the universe and its Purposeful Designer would accept me as a partner and co-creator for numerous sacred missions, such as the writing of this book.

Years ago, I remember asking a simple question to my Sunday School class while teaching a course on C.S. Lewis's *The Screwtape Letters*[15]. I asked, "What do you believe is your primary reason for being on this planet?" I'll never forget the answer a dear friend, a humble countryman, gave from the back of the room. He said, "That's easy, Ski. It's to get to the other side of this life, into heaven, and to take as many people as I encounter with me." There was no need for me to teach this sophisticated, complex book to this man; he already knew the most important answer. He had nothing to learn from me but much to teach me.

While it brings me joy to know you've taken this journey with me, I must ask one more thing of you. Our world is in desperate need of balance. Mahatma Gandhi said, "Truth is God and God is truth." His peaceful rebellion, satyagraha, or 'holding onto truth,' advocated for civil disobedience methods like boycotts and strikes, rejecting any form of violence, even in self-defense. Martin Luther King Jr., a revered figure in the U.S. civil rights movement, adopted Gandhi's methods.

Regardless of whether we have a deep faith or even belief in God, we must participate in the struggle for truth and consciousness. If we speak words of truth and live a life based on truth, or at least the quest for truth, we are working as co-creators with Divine Purpose. This way, our reality becomes one of love and truth and embodies these sacred characteristics.

You may be wondering, "What can I do? I'm just one person." Let me share a lesson I learned early in my life. A prominent board member of a startup company I founded once said, "Ski, your best characteristic is that you're too damn stupid to know what you can't do, so you're not afraid to try anything." May we all be too stupid to know what we can't do so, we can act to make this a more beautiful and mindful world.

And if you're thinking, "I'm just in this little corner of the world. What can I do?" I want you to remember the story and impact of my beautiful Grandma Chilton. For me, she was the most influential person in my life. We lived way back in the country, and I spent 12 to 14 hours a day working in the tobacco fields. My Grandma Chilton fixed lunch for me every day. Despite having severe osteoporosis, I never heard her complain. Despite having a very large family of almost one hundred aunts, uncles, and cousins, I never saw her angry or say a negative word about one person. Grandma Chilton lived to be 100 years old, and up until age 95, she mowed her one-acre lawn and tended her 1/4-acre garden. Every Sunday for lunch, there were no less than 20 people at her table.

My little Chilton family did well by world standards. We have lots of doctors, nurses, professionals, entrepreneurs, and other extremely successful people. Most importantly, this is a family of very loving spirits. I think if we were each individually asked what most influenced our success, our answer would be the gentleness, love, resilience, and spirit of Grandma Chilton. She was an angel among us. The ripple effects of her love and gentle heart permeate each of us and are a constant source of strength. These characteristics and their impact on me made this very book possible.

Grandma Chilton was a little woman from Stokes County, North Carolina, that no one will ever know about. However, her mindfulness, love, and strength will live on for generations through us and you, if you are reading this book. If you feel you can do nothing, my call is simple. *Live like Grandma Chilton, and you, along with the blessings shining from your beautiful essence, will change the world!*

This is my earnest plea for you. Practice mindfulness in your own life, and create an atmosphere of love, understanding, and compassion for those around you. This world needs your love so badly.

Be blessed, my dear friends. I am deeply honored you have spent this time with me, and I hope to meet you all someday soon…ski.

# Part 2:

# The CAST Process: Thirteen Weeks of Inspiration, Mindful/Meditation, and Self-Reflection Practices

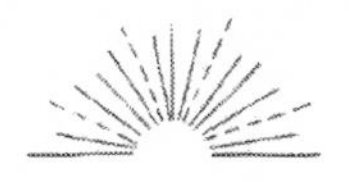

**Introduction**

I sincerely hope and pray that this book has so far been instrumental in initiating a life-altering journey for you. As potent as these words may be, I must emphasize that based on my own experience, attaining higher levels of awareness is challenging without dedicating considerable time to meditation. This understanding is precisely why I've included 13 weeks of mindful practices, including inspirational readings, meditations, and self-reflections corresponding to the four CAST steps. I strongly encourage you to invest significant time in each practice, up to a week if possible. Through this commitment and repeated practice, the transformation will begin to take root.

I hope you trust that I will always be honest with you, so allow me to begin with a confession. A decade ago, I approached meditation as an utter skeptic. In my mind, those who practiced it, particularly those in the Western world, were simply new-age enthusiasts, wasting away their days in a state of Zen, accomplishing little to nothing. Yes, it may sound harsh, but to be honest, I hope to connect with those of you starting from a similar viewpoint.

The practice of meditation boasts a rich history, spanning around ten thousand years, with the earliest forms stemming from Taoist China and Buddhist India and later spreading to other Eastern nations. In the West, meditation techniques were established by Plotinus in the third century, followed by Saint Augustine and subsequent Christian mystics. Historical evidence also suggests that Judaism embraced the practice of meditation, a tradition that expanded in the Middle Ages with the advent of Kabbalistic practices. Similar techniques found a home in Islamic practices, notably within Sufism. As a rational thinker, I was daunted by the sheer multitude of meditation schools and methodologies arising from these traditions. How could I even attempt to meditate if I didn't fully grasp the roots of these varying meditation traditions?

And that was just the beginning. The Western world introduced an abundance of meditation techniques that further overwhelmed me. Zen meditation, mindfulness meditation, mantra meditation, yoga meditations, Taoist meditations, and contemplative prayer were only the tip of the iceberg. Add to that the host of New Age terminologies – "nirvana, noble truths, om, third eye, dharma, chakras, energy points" – none of which sat comfortably with my logical, reductionist, scientific mind. In an attempt to learn, I joined several meditation groups, only to encounter individuals I can best describe as "militant meditators," who asserted that the 'correct' philosophy and techniques were essential for calming the mind and achieving enlightenment. Frankly, many seemed like control freaks who had merely shifted their normal Western obsessions to meditation.

However, after a few months of engaging with meditation and yoga groups, I stumbled upon the app Insight Timer. I spoke about it in Chapter 4. It offered an extensive network of practitioners and over

70,000 guided meditations. I began exploring these, trying to meditate alongside them. To be honest, I didn't resonate with most of the practitioners, mainly due to the issues previously stated. But then, I found a select few that deeply touched my core, leading me to delve into their favorites and discover even more inspiring voices. One of my initial, profound discoveries was a practitioner named Sarah Blondin. Her 8-minute meditation, "Learning to Surrender," moved me to my core. Others must have been moved by it as well as it has been listened to on Insight Timer more than 2.8 million times since 2016. After that, I was driven to unearth the potential gold mine that I sensed could be tapped from meditating.

I also experimented with other meditation apps, uncovering additional paths to peace and meaning. Gradually, over two years, I began to comprehend the critical concepts and meditative practices that held meaning for me, as well as those that offered the most potent capacity to calm my mind, confront my core issues, and connect me to something far greater than myself. This beautiful journey had an immensely positive impact on my life.

Over time, I began to sense that my meditation journey was progressing in four beautiful, overlapping steps, each allowing me to move to the next. It was as if I was hiking a magnificent mountain range, and once I progressed to the top of one glorious peak, there was a brilliant new one right in front of me. I could not believe the marvelous spiritual insight that traversing each peak provided and how, collectively, this path had completely transformed me. I remember the day almost 4 years later when I looked back to better discern the meanings of the steps I had taken to get to this point. Looking back at the peaks climbed from the highest peak, I could see before me 4 distinct steps, which I gave the name CAST. At this point in the book, you are familiar with these steps as *Awakening **C**onsciousness, Deepening **A**wareness, The Art of **S**urrender, and **T**rust the Journey*, all detailed in the preceding chapters. I love that the acronym for the technique is CAST, a term that signifies the action of discarding or getting rid of something you don't need. It's beautifully apt. By employing the CAST Process, we're actively shedding all that hinders us or acts as a barrier to the light of our innate happiness. However, CAST also means to shape or mold into something beautifully different. We become "a new creature: old things are passed away; behold, all things are become new."[31] I do hope you find these 13 weekly practices deeply meaningful and transformative.

Each weekly topic will begin with an inspirational reading corresponding to a meditation/mindfulness practice, followed by a time of self-reflection journaling. Throughout the week, revisit the inspirational reading multiple times. Each inspirational reading is an opportunity to delve deeper into the meaning of the words. By mid-week, I hope these passages will have facilitated a profound, internal revelation transcending words and standard reflections. Perhaps they might even instill a sense of delving into the realms of the mystical and sacred.

The reading will be supplemented weekly by a meditation/mindfulness session, initially lasting just a few minutes. By the 5$^{th}$ week, these sessions will gradually extend to 10 to 20-minute durations. After each meditation, I encourage you to spend time journaling in the self-reflection section of the book. Some days, this may simply be a couple of sentences or a succinct paragraph, while other times, you might feel compelled to write more extensively to capture your feelings and experiences. If the space provided in this book proves insufficient, consider obtaining a separate notebook to chronicle all your thoughts and experiences.

If your journey mirrors mine, the words you inscribe in this book and your additional notebook will become precious gems. You are chronicling a sacred journey towards heightened awareness and joy in the most important areas of your life. Through this process, you are documenting a span of 13 weeks (equivalent to 3 months) during which you experienced an awakening and unearthed the happiness that has resided within you all along.

*Be blessed, my dear friends, as you embark upon Part 2 of this sacred journey.*

# Step 1 -

# Awakening Consciousness

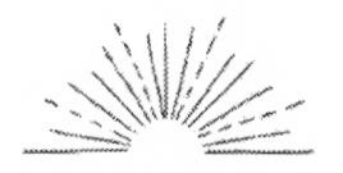

## Week 1-What is Meditation and Why Should I Do It?

**Inspirational Reading:**

What is meditation, you ask? Why do I stir myself from the comfort of my bed every morning at the ungodly hour of 5:30 a.m. to engage in this practice? As I said above in the beginning, a healthy dose of skepticism colored my initial perspective on meditation. I was amused by the obscure jargon and practices that swirled around it. It all seemed like New Age mumbo-jumbo to my rational, scientifically-trained mind.

Yet, I couldn't ignore the burgeoning body of scientific evidence supporting the benefits of meditation. Over 9,600 scientific articles were published by 2022, up from a mere 191 in 2010 and just 7 in 2000. The data provide a compelling case for its potential to alleviate a wide array of ailments from cardiovascular disease and mental health disorders to aging. *Now, that was something that piqued my interest and got my respect!*

I had previously written about the incredible power of the unconscious mind in my book, *The Rewired Brain*[5], and how its unchecked influence often wreaks havoc in our lives. But for me, there was one major question that remained unanswered. Was there a solution to our habitually-devastating unconscious minds, and if so, what was it?

Throughout the process of writing that book, I started to question my own identity. Was I simply a collection of my feelings, emotions, thoughts, actions, and reactions? I came to realize that these were facets of my unconscious *Me*, my small self. This thought led me to ponder whether there was a deeper, true *Self,* an *I* within my being, struggling to break free from the prison erected by my unconscious mind and the circumstances it constantly creates.

The burning question then became how could I discover my true *Self*? Where do I look amidst the chaos and noise my unconscious mind generates? I was overwhelmed, on the brink of despair, because I could not find an answer to this most important question.

That's when I began to seriously consider mindfulness meditation. To say the journey has been straightforward would not be honest. I was a scientist on a desperate quest to find a rational approach to calm my irrational, unconscious mind. At first, I found the concept of meditation elusive and hard to grasp. This was especially the case with the distraction of eclectic belief systems of New Age practitioners who seemed to borrow practices and terminology from a variety of religious traditions, including Buddhism, Hinduism, Taoism, Paganism, and Shamanism, along with influences from psychology, science, and other varied sources. But with time and practice, I began to understand the sacred beauty of mindfulness practices, including meditation.

Perhaps more than anything else, meditation brought me peace. It was the kind of peace that, in the words of the Apostle Paul, "transcends all understanding," even on the worst days, amidst the greatest losses.

I then started to weave the important teachings and principles from other spiritual practices into my existing spiritual framework. I drew heavily not only from the teachings of Jesus, but Buddha as well, and the contemplative wisdom traditions of old. I was particularly impacted by

*Living Buddha, Living Christ*[32] written by the Vietnamese monk, Thich Nhat Hanh. Published in 1995, it's a reflective and contemplative text that aims to find common ground between Buddhism and Christianity. The book is highly respected, and I particularly appreciated its interfaith dialogue and thoughtful comparisons between the teachings of Jesus and the Buddha.

The core of the book lies in its exploration of how both spiritual traditions, although originating in different cultural contexts, with distinctive rituals and practices, speak to universal human concerns. It maintains that both Buddhism and Christianity offer valuable insights that can help people live more compassionate, mindful, and meaningful lives. Thich Nhat Hanh emphasized the importance of "mindful living," a concept deeply rooted in Buddhism, and pointed out that Jesus's teachings were very mindful and deeply present in each moment.

During this process, I discovered that modern science and ancient contemplative wisdom traditions could interact and enrich each other in extraordinarily beautiful ways. They were not mutually exclusive but rather complementary, each shedding light on the other. This realization, I believe, is driving the current surge of mindfulness-based programs across various medical disciplines and spiritual practices.

Now, let me share three key principles I wish I'd known at the beginning of my meditation journey. First, I quickly began to sense that a primary objective of mindful meditation was not so much to discover who you are but rather who you are not. This might seem confusing initially, but bear with me – it will become clearer as we continue this journey together. Essentially, the unconscious mind drives much of our daily emotions, giving rise to looping thoughts that drive us crazy. Initially, we think that is who we are. But it is not! There is a true *I* underneath all the noise, but the only way to find that *I* is to peel back the layers of the unconscious *Me*.

Second, the crux of this journey is learning to become your own inner observer. By observing the thoughts and reactions that arise from your fears, emotions, and resentments in a curious and non-judgmental manner, you'll begin to discern their true nature. You will understand they are not you. Imagine your thoughts as clouds passing across the sky. Some clouds (or thoughts) are large and stormy, others may be fluffy and pleasant, and some may be wispy and almost transparent. But no matter their size or shape, they all share one key characteristic: they are temporary and transient, just passing by in the sky of your mind. They cannot be you because they are temporary, transient, and impermanent. You are the one who observes the clouds, but you are not the clouds themselves.

Finally, don't be surprised if you start feeling something different, something inexplicable, as you delve deeper into meditation. It might feel like you've been transported to an entirely different world. I ran college track, and I vividly remember the "runner's high." I felt a similar "meditation high" that was so soothing during my practices.

That's enough for this week. Let's now go meditate, journal, and remember – relax and enjoy! Please be patient and compassionate with yourselves. This process is different for everyone. Feeling any change may take weeks and months beyond the 13 weeks provided here. In fact, you may want to repeat any or all the weekly meditations. Most of all, remember that this is a mystical, sacred lifetime journey, not a magical "quick fix."

**Meditation and Mindfulness Practice:**

Let me invite you to step into the realms of silence, the home of stillness. Find a quiet and peaceful spot where you won't be easily distracted. You can sit on a cushion, chair, or even lie down, as long as you can maintain alertness. Five minutes is all it takes. Strive for mental calmness, and let's uncover what revelations lie within. Once the five minutes are up, open your eyes and put pen to paper below in your journaling. Note your experience, struggles in achieving stillness, unexpected surprises, feelings, and thoughts. You are likely to be surprised at how foreign stillness feels.

Expect your mind to roam aimlessly or to feel different emotions. It's okay. This is part of the process. Your mind, with its ceaseless wandering, is revealing something about you. Isn't that a discovery? Take a moment to consider this unpredictable drifting of thoughts, and let the revelation sink into you. What you are experiencing is largely the conscious output of your unconscious mind. However, the mere fact you're aware of your mental meanderings, your emotional turmoil, or your battle with stillness indicates there is calmness and a source of that calmness within you. This awareness is a form of stillness where your *I*, your true *Self*, resides.

When you get to the second half of the week, repeat the exercise, expanding the length to maybe 8-10 minutes if you wish. But this time, focus on the content of your wandering mind. At the same time, feel the stillness that empowers you to be aware of the mind's travels. This experience of stillness within is what you'll continue to work on, and it will magnify the more time is spent there. As it grows, it will become a mirror reflecting more about you. Or, more precisely, it will introduce you to the workings of your unconscious mind and the capacity of your true *Self* to observe it.

In these initial weeks, I urge you to keep your expectations low. You're not seeking sensational revelations, flashes of light, or divine insights. Instead, you're here just to observe and take in everything your awareness presents, no matter how ordinary. Even the tiniest realizations, such as an itch on your arm, a desire to change posture, or what you are having for dinner tonight, all matter and are all being observed. It's not about what you're aware of but the capacity to be aware. As your awareness grows and improves, your stillness deepens. And as your stillness deepens, you begin to change. This change is more than mere knowledge. There is a mysterious transformative power within us that brings about the change.

Remember, it's okay if you find this intense. Feel free to take a day off or repeat the exercise as needed. The journey to discovering yourself isn't a race. It's a beautiful dance, one that you learn with gentle, nonjudgmental practice.

**Self-Reflection:** What surprised you about this exercise? How did you feel? What insights did you learn from your thoughts? Write down some thoughts and emotions you observed in just a word or two. Don't give them too much power.

## Week 2-The Tools and Anchors of Mindfulness and Meditation

### Inspirational Reading:

When I first started meditating, I found myself bombarded with countless questions. What does it mean to observe or find the Observer? How can I negotiate the persistent cacophony of sounds and distractions around me? Most crucially, how do I tame this rampant, untamed mind of mine? And this talk of breathing... am I supposed to master a specific technique?

Through a course of trial and error and an array of techniques, I realized that most meditation forms share a common element. They require us to focus on a reference point, abstain from assigning value judgments, and refocus our attention when the mind inevitably begins to wander. These 'attention anchors,' as they are called, have become my lifesavers amid the turbulent seas of my mind.

Let me underscore that one meditation style or anchor isn't innately superior to another. It's about finding what resonates with you and suits your evolving circumstances. For instance, focusing on my breath has been my key meditation anchor during my day-to-day life. When it comes to breathing, I've discovered that it's best for me to let it flow naturally. You might gravitate towards techniques that slow down your breath, such as the 4-8 or the 5-3-7 patterns. Identify where the sensation of breath is most pronounced for you. It might be the nostrils, the belly, or the chest. There's no right or wrong here, just what feels right to you.

Several years ago, when a severe accident left me with a fractured pelvis bound to a wheelchair, body scans turned into my sanctuary. Paying attention to different body parts, especially those experiencing pain, helped me manage my discomfort. It also provided a robust shield from the emotional turmoil accompanying an uncertain future. Body scans continue to be a powerful anchor for me. Thoughts find it hard to interrupt me when my entire attention is on the energy emerging from my fingertips or toes or feeling the rhythm of my heartbeat. Body scans are also my go-to when I need assistance falling asleep. Some people find grounding at the contact points between their body and the surface, whether it's the floor, a mat, a chair, or a cushion, an excellent way of establishing a connection with the body, managing discomfort, and providing a focus point for the mind.

Sounds such as music or the harmonies of nature are also valuable anchors. If the music doesn't distract you and fosters a positive mindset, it can enhance your meditation. Nature is a big one for me. The breeze on my cheek and the soothing rustle of leaves or birds chirping quickly transport me to another world. Visualizing nature or recalling serene outdoor experiences can effectively anchor your mind. I often gaze at a majestic palm tree I've named 'Divine Presence' that sits just beyond my backyard. For me, it is a symbol of God's presence.

And then there are mantras. These can be sacred messages or sounds that guide the mind toward inner balance and wellbeing. Repeating mantras can help purify, pacify, and transform your mind and heart, serving as an impactful tool to effect changes in your psyche and body. I am particularly fond of positive self-talk mantras. Phrases like "It's okay, you've had a tough day," "Anyone in your shoes would feel the same," "There's nothing wrong with feeling this way," and "I'm proud of you."

Mixing various anchors can sometimes provide powerful and soothing meditative experiences, particularly in challenging situations. I love to take my daily walks by focusing on my breathing, then tuning in to the sounds and sights of nature without identifying them by name. It doesn't take long to become fully absorbed in the stillness of nature around me.

Meditation, with all its various anchors, equips us with tools to navigate our inner world, embrace tranquility, and face life's highs and lows with equanimity. That's enough for this week. Now let's go meditate and journal… and remember – relax and enjoy!

**Meditation and Mindfulness Practice:**

For the first few days of this week, I invite you to participate in a body scan meditation for 5 minutes. Now, you might already be acquainted with an array of meditation tools and techniques, and some may be beginners. It doesn't matter where you are on your journey. The body scan meditation is one of the most elemental and effective practices, a wonderful starting point for any novice, and a powerful touchstone for more seasoned practitioners.

Find a place where you're most comfortable. It could be a chair, a soft rug, or even your own cozy bed. Settle yourself in a position that allows for relaxation yet alertness. Rest your palms facing upwards and gently close your eyes. This is your space, your moment. Start by taking a few slow breaths, inhaling deeply, and exhaling with a slow, soothing rhythm.

Begin the body scan by bringing your conscious awareness to your feet. Feel the sensation. It might be a slight tickle, a warm enveloping coziness, a coolness, or simply pressure against the surface. Don't judge if you don't feel much. Remember, this exercise is not about feeling a particular sensation but enhancing awareness.

As you continue, slowly move your focus from your feet to your ankles, calves, knees, thighs, and hips. Take your time as you navigate through your entire body, experiencing and acknowledging each part with non-judgmental awareness. When you've reached the crown of your head, it's time to embrace the entire existence of your body. Feel life humming within you and breathe deeply, enjoying the whole experience.

In the second part of the week, let's move to another awareness anchor, your breath. Focus on the breath, but don't try to control or manipulate it in any way. Let it flow naturally. Feel the air moving through your nostrils on the in-breath and out-breath. Remember, this is not about altering the breath but observing it, tuning into its rhythm, its touch.

Every time you find your mind wandering, gently bring it back to your breath. Persistence is key here. Gradually, with practice, you will notice the warmth or coolness of the air as it flows in and out. As your awareness deepens, you will notice many things, perhaps even your heartbeat. Remember, the goal here isn't perfection but progress. Keep returning to the breath to anchor awareness.

By the end of week two, you will have experience with two very important tools that provide great assistance as you continue to enhance your awareness of your thoughts and emotions.

**Self-Reflection:** What piqued your interest during these practices? Did you enjoy both techniques? Was one more effective or enjoyable than the other?

## Week 3-Our Monkey Minds

### Inspirational Reading:

Just imagine it - the Monkey Mind. A ceaseless chatterbox, constantly swinging from one thought branch to another, akin to a monkey traversing from tree to tree in the jungle. Does this sound or feel familiar? Yet, it's important to remember that the existence of this monkey mind isn't abnormal. It is, in fact, quite normal and a result of evolutionary, experiential, and societal programming centered in places of fear, competition, loneliness, and past and future events. Our mind is compelled to warn us about everything that could go wrong while also fueling our ego to ensure the survival of our 'precious genes.'

Our friend Buddha, over two and a half millennia ago, beautifully encapsulated the concept of this Monkey Mind. He suggested that just like a monkey grabbing a branch and letting it go only to seize another, our thoughts, minds, or consciousness arise and continually disappear day and night. While his wisdom is timeless, we're left wondering - why does the monkey get to rule the roost up there in our minds? Aren't we conscious beings supposed to be the ones in command?

Diving into the field of neuroscience, we find a startling truth. An estimated greater than 95 percent of our feelings, emotions, and fears happen unconsciously, slipping beneath our conscious awareness. But that doesn't mean we don't experience them. It's rather like being in a pitch-black forest, emotionally overwhelmed by unseen threats and unheard cries. This unconscious chatter feeds into our conscious thoughts, contributing to the ceaseless activity of the Monkey Mind.

These unconscious thoughts are incredibly powerful, and they vie for our attention. We're constantly under a barrage of confusion, self-doubt, and anxiety stemming from our Monkey Mind. The noise from our unconscious minds leaves us in perpetual unrest. We're trapped in a cycle of rehashing past mistakes and conversations and projecting these fears and confusions onto an uncertain and risky future. In this loop, no time or energy is left to experience the present moment. *But is there another way?*

There is, and that is why I've included these meditation practices. We desperately need tools that allow our conscious minds to regulate this primitive system, which is so easily manipulated by external forces and causing us distress. Mindful meditation is a powerful tool that allows us to observe but not attach to the thoughts of our Monkey Mind. All these thoughts are vying for our attention. But we, our true *Selves*, our *I*'s, have the capacity to say no.

The thoughts of the Monkey Mind are asking us to hop aboard their train, but if we do, they will inevitably control us and block our path to happiness. Through these practices, we are now developing the capacity to sense and recognize the thought trains as they approach. Standing on the platform as the train rushes towards us, we find within our *I* the capacity to say, "Not today," and watch as the thoughts recede into the distance. I promise you can do this.

**Meditation and Mindfulness Practice:**

Practicing mindfulness meditation is one of the most effective ways to manage a Monkey Mind. In week three, we will combine the two practices from the previous two weeks to address our Monkey Minds. If possible, do this practice for 10 minutes at least 4 to 5 times this week.

Find a chair or put a firm pillow on the ground for this exercise. Sit up with your shoulders relaxed, your palms facing upwards, or in any comfortable position, and bring a big smile to your face. Smiling has been shown to trigger the parasympathetic nervous system, releasing neurotransmitters like dopamine, endorphins, and serotonin, often called "feel-good" hormones. They not only make us feel happier but also work as natural pain relievers and antidepressants, and they can help reduce physical or emotional stress. This also leads to the reduction of heart rate and blood pressure and promotes a state of equilibrium. So, smile often whether you are meditating or not.

Now, let's gently close our eyes and begin by focusing on the stillness, the present moment. With the anchor of breathing, you have gained a powerful new tool to learn to observe your thoughts without getting caught up in them. Begin to notice your breath. Here, we will use deep, slow breathing exercises to keep us calm and help bring our minds back to the present moment. Now, for the next 10 minutes, when you notice your thoughts racing, move your focus back to your breath. Feel its rhythm and the sensation of the air entering and leaving your body.

In my words, here's what the progression of your awareness might look like. I am conscious of my breath... Aware of my inhalation and exhalation... Suddenly, I realize I am absorbed in a thought... Fully engrossed in thinking. *I*, my awareness realizes it moved away from stillness. *I* gently and nonjudgmentally say to myself, "thinking... thinking... thinking" or "not today…not today…not today." This instantly moves me back to my breath and observing. Then, if an unexpected sound breaks my silence, I say to myself, "listening... listening... listening," and this reminds me to move back to my breath and stillness. If I feel irritated, I acknowledge my "irritation... irritation... irritation," and so on.

In this practice, the wandering mind isn't viewed as a distraction or problem if you are cognizant of its shifting focus. Once you've perceived this change, stay with the new object of your attention for a moment (whether it's thinking, listening, or feeling) before returning to the primary object of your focus: your breath.

The more you engage in this exercise, the more adept you will become at detecting not just the shift of your attention but even the desire of the initial impulse to turn your focus elsewhere. The more refined your awareness becomes, the more you will recognize these subtleties within yourself. These shifts and impulses are just as crucial to your self-understanding as are the more prominent thoughts and emotions. By consistently practicing this mindful awareness, you will become more and more acquainted with the ebb and flow of your inner world.

**Self-Reflection:** What surprised you about this exercise? Were you able to recognize when your attention moved away and then move it back to your breath? How did that make you feel?

# Step 2 –

# Deepening Awareness

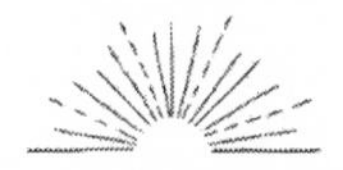

## Week 4-Negative Bias and Negative Self-Talk

**Inspirational Reading:**

Negativity bias and negative self-talk are phenomena frequently observed in humans. Even when we experience good and bad events of equivalent intensity, negative thoughts, emotions, or social interactions related to unpleasant, harmful, or traumatic events tend to impact us more profoundly than neutral or positive ones. This is why we often find ourselves ruminating over an insult or dwelling on our mistakes. Criticisms typically hold more weight than compliments, and we pay more attention to bad news than good news. Traumatic experiences are usually remembered more vividly than positive ones.

Why is this the case? Again, it all comes down to our evolutionary history, our unconscious lizard brain. For our early ancestors, focusing on the dangerous, harmful, and negative elements of their environment was a matter of survival. Those more attuned to these threats and gave them greater attention were more likely to manage their environment, survive, and pass on their genes.

As I've emphasized throughout this book, evolution's primary objective wasn't our happiness, and mother nature is indifferent to our emotional state. In fact, from an evolutionary perspective, it was more beneficial for us to be unhappy if that compelled us to out-compete our rivals and protect our tribe. Despite what the news and social media suggest, we no longer need to be in a constant state of high alert.

Negativity bias still plays a pivotal role in how our unconscious minds operate. We often expect the worst in others, particularly in close relationships. When we anticipate a negative reaction from our partner, our defenses instinctively rise. We remember our partner's negative comments more vividly than positive ones, or we transfer the negative personality traits of individuals from previous relationships into our current ones. Negativity bias also affects our decisions. When we expect a negative outcome, it can severely limit our choices and dampen our joy.

This bias is further reinforced when coupled with negative self-talk. As mentioned in Chapter 5, our words don't merely serve as a communication tool; they're a force that shapes our reality. Our minds often can't discern between what's said in jest and what's serious or whether the words come from us or someone else. This ambiguity turns even mild self-deprecation into a source of negative self-perceptions. By switching our self-talk from negative to positive, we can transform not just our mindset but our entire life. Positive self-talk encourages us to perceive ourselves more favorably by boosting our confidence, dismantling our self-imposed restrictions, and unearthing the happiness within us.

Through conscious awareness, we can identify this negativity bias and self-talk and choose not to engage with it, whether during meditation or daily life. If we are fixated on past mistakes that we can't change, we struggle with self-forgiveness. As someone who's made significant errors, I've learned that my lizard brain was in charge at the time of those mistakes, leading me to make the only choice available given my level of consciousness or, more accurately, unconsciousness. Now, through a lot of self-reflection, meditation, and awareness, I believe that I have a better capacity to pause and move away from unconscious reactions, and this process allows me to make better decisions.

With others, especially those we love, conscious awareness lets us identify our negative biases and examine our feelings with curiosity before we act or react. This mindfulness encourages us to be more compassionate and forgiving with others. It invites us to stop expecting the worst.

Starting with today's practice, I want you to pay attention to the types of thoughts and self-talk running through your mind. Recognize feelings and words like "I shouldn't have done that" or "I can't believe they did that to me." Observe these negative thoughts and words with curiosity. Ask yourself, "Where are these thoughts coming from?" Understand that thoughts and words, especially negative ones, are constantly vying for your attention. Simply say, "Sorry, not today," and watch them float away harmlessly.

**Meditation and Mindfulness Practice:**

As I discussed in Chapter 5 and the reading above, one of the greatest challenges we face in our journey to self-discovery is the relentless negative narratives and self-talk. Despite success, I have dealt with this feeling of unworthiness and imposter syndrome for most of my life. It has been a constant background chatter that has often diminished my sense of *Self*, joy, and peace. In the first few days of this week, we will address this in a meditation exercise and then, in the last part of the week, in daily living.

For the meditation, I invite you to take on the following exercise for 10-15 minutes each day. Find a quiet place where you will be undisturbed. Sit comfortably, close your eyes, and take a few deep, calming breaths. Allow yourself to be soaked in the moment, anchored in the present.

Now, begin to listen to your inner dialogue. Don't try to change anything just yet. Allow any thoughts to arise, even if they're negative or self-deprecating. As they do, acknowledge them without judgment. Say to yourself, “I notice that I’m having the thought that I’m [insert negative thought].”

Once you’ve acknowledged the thought, imagine the negative thought as a leaf floating down a gentle stream. This powerful visualization helps us remember that these destructive thoughts are temporary if we don’t engage with them and leave them alone. They will pass, just like the leaf will eventually float out of sight. Watch as your negative thought floats away, and let it go.

After the thought has drifted away, redirect your focus back to your breath. Feel the sensation of the air entering and exiting your lungs. Notice the rise and fall of your chest. This acts as an anchor, keeping you rooted in the present.

As negative thoughts reappear, which they likely will, simply repeat the process. Acknowledge the thought without judgment, imagine it floating away on a leaf, and return your attention to your breath.

Watch your mind in the second half of the week as you do your daily activities. You may employ the same technique as in meditation. Allow any negative thoughts to arise, acknowledge them without judgment, don’t engage with them, and leave them alone. They will pass, just like the leaf will eventually float out of sight.

Remember, this is not about forcibly clearing your mind of all thoughts. Instead, it’s about becoming a compassionate observer of your inner dialogue, understanding that thoughts are transient, and learning not to get swept away by negative narratives.

I have another technique, although I’m not certain mindfulness practitioners would approve it. I used to walk into a room or situation, and my thoughts would instantly shout, “This sucks!” I then realized that there was no validity to that statement. My negative bias was kicking in when there was absolutely nothing wrong. When I do this now, and I still do, I just laugh at myself and ask the question, “Ski, what is your mind talking about? Could you specifically tell me what sucks?” The true answer usually is that nothing sucks, and I really am living a magical life.

Now, I acknowledge that there may be situations that may be uncomfortable or undesirable, but in the greater scheme of life, they typically don't rise to the level of judging your life in such a negative way. Remember, nothing remains as it is. It will pass just as the leaf floats down the river. All of this shuts down Mr. "Lizard Brain" for a while, but he usually tries again another time. Unfortunately, he is very persistent, but that being said, he tends to wear down as we ignore him.

Keep practicing these, and you'll become more resilient to negative self-talk over time. The narrative and resulting talk will lose its grip on you and allow you to see yourself and your world in a more positive, compassionate, loving light. In all these exercises, please remember, it's not about perfection. It is about progress and cultivating an awareness that leads to a deeper understanding of you and the joy within you.

**Self-Reflection:** Did you have negative thoughts? Were you able to watch them appear and disappear? Perhaps make a list of the negative thoughts. Then, strike a line through that thought and replace it with a positive thought.

## Week 5-My Pain Source

### Inspirational Reading:

During an ordinary week, I feel dull aches in my heart a few times. I'm caught in uncertainty and chaos or nagging loneliness. When I wake up some mornings, I am frightened by my horrible nightmares, the realization of all the things that could go wrong, the thought that someone will figure out that I am unworthy of all this success, or the unthinkable fear that something awful will happen to one of the eight children and one granddaughter my wife and I share.

These feelings used to overwhelm me. But now, with my newly acquired awareness and ability to come back to the present moment, they have less power to rule my well-being. I am better equipped to witness my fears, surrender them, and flip back to the present in a matter of just a few minutes.

Much of this paralyzing fear and uncertainty comes from what I call the "pain source." Because of its importance to emotional health, modern psychologists and spiritual teachers have given this idea several different names, most famously the "pain body" by Eckhart Tolle. Understanding the nature of the pain source and its impact is crucial and thus the focus of the three chapters in Step 2- Deepening Awareness.

To find peace and happiness, it is vital to learn the characteristics and function of the pain source and the role it plays in emotional dysfunction, addiction, and reactivity. The pain source is constructed of past painful and fearful memories that we have suppressed or not accepted or dealt with. These include physical and emotional trauma(s), early childhood trauma and conditioning, childhood relationships with parents and others, failures, mistakes, broken relationships, difficult life transitions, and the collective pain and fear of society around us. Specially, Chapter 4 focuses on childhood trauma, given its great capacity to devastate our lives. I talk about how this inflicts our lives with destructive and often unexpected reactions and perspectives and how 'shadow' work can help uncover and heal these dark places from our innocent past.

This pain source can be a devastating internal flame that creates unconscious feelings, emotions, and sensations like anger, fear, and chaos stemming from repressed or expressed memories. This generates conscious stress, anxiety, and incessant thoughts that serve as catalysts for countless other thoughts and unsubstantiated narratives, making us great conquerors over those who hurt us but, more often, an unnecessarily punished, innocent victim.

The pain source can remain as a dormant yet active volcano for prolonged periods of time. However, when the pressure becomes too great, it will explode, destroying relationships and any joy and peace that we have found. After such an explosion, we often look around and wonder what the hell happened. How could I have acted this way? The more aware person wonders what happened to them and where all that anger came from?

Recognizing the pain source with curiosity about unexplained painful thoughts will immediately begin to reduce the destructive power of the pain source. For me, curiosity was a particularly effective healing tool. I wondered why my thinking was so consistently focused on certain topics. The thoughts could almost always be traced back to feelings of being unloved or being unworthy. Daily meditations enhanced my capacity for alertness and inquisitiveness, thereby defusing the bombs waiting to explode from my unconscious mind and releasing me from my addiction to my past.

**Meditation and Mindfulness Practice:**

For a fuller description of my experience with 'shadow' work and what you might expect, please reread the first part of Chapter 4. 'Shadow' work is exploring your inner darkness, or 'Shadow Self'. As defined by Carl Jung, the 'Shadow Self' is the part of us that we may try to reject or hide (repress) from ourselves - this could be certain feelings, desires, fears, or behaviors that typically have an early childhood origin. This type of work can be intense, so it's important to approach it with kindness and patience and perhaps do this meditation at most a couple of times during this week. This time may be made up by journaling what you find.

If you suspect abusive childhood trauma, it is important to seek the support of a counselor or therapist before going too deep. As you see from Chapter 4, I had no idea I would find the devastated, scared, incredibly sad version of my childhood self when I started this work. This caused great initial pain and shock to my adult self. That being said, it led to the eventual healing of my adult self. As I suggested earlier, I would highly recommend the talks and meditations by Catherine Liggett[11] on this topic.

Here's a 10-15 minute meditation you can use to begin your 'shadow' work. I intentionally will not push too far with this meditation, and you may stop at any time.

Begin by finding a quiet and comfortable space to meditate without interruptions. Sit or lie down, close your eyes, and take a few deep, calming breaths. As you exhale, let go of the tension in your body and mind.

Start by turning your attention inward. Ask yourself, "What parts of myself am I avoiding or denying?" or "Is there something I am hiding from myself?" These can be thoughts, feelings, memories, or behaviors you're uncomfortable with or ashamed of. Perhaps you find a fear of abandonment or being alone or being left behind. As you read in Chapter 4, for me, this was an exaggerated feeling of shame from day-to-day disappointments.

Once something comes to mind, don't rush to judge or dismiss it. Instead, observe it with curiosity. Remember, these 'shadow' aspects aren't "bad" or "wrong". They're simply parts of your full human experience. You are also in a very sacred space where you can interact with and soothe your childhood self and integrate this part of you with your adult self.

The most surprising part of this practice was my capacity to directly communicate with my childhood self with words such as "I am here for you, little buddy," "You've gone through so much." "Anyone would feel the way you do given what you have experienced." "I love you and will never leave you." I found that I could even ask questions of my childhood *Self*, "What do you need, sweet boy?" "How can I comfort you?"

Acknowledge any feelings that arise as you face your 'shadow self'. You might feel discomfort, fear, or sadness, and that's okay. You may cry as I did under that tree on our campus. It's all part of the process. Breathe into these feelings, offering them and yourself love, compassion, and understanding. If this experience is too intense or overwhelming, stop and take some deep breaths. Perhaps you will try again later, or not.

Now, consider how these shadow aspects might have been trying to protect or serve you, even in flawed ways. For example, if you often feel jealousy or believe you are never good enough, that might stem from being neglected or undervalued as a child. This perspective can help you approach your 'shadow self' with more kindness and less judgment.

In the final minute, take a few more deep breaths and express gratitude to yourself for being with your shadow today. Gently bring your awareness back to your surroundings and open your eyes when you're ready. Take your time. Remember, it took me two hours to be ready to walk back to my office after my initial experience with 'shadow' work.

As described above, 'shadow' work can be an intense process, and it's not necessary to rush it. In fact, you may only want to do this exercise a couple of times in Week 5 or not at all if it is too intense. Be gentle with yourself, and I strongly recommend seeking the support of a counselor or therapist if needed.

**Self-Reflection:** Are you okay? Are you surprised by what you found? I find it often helps (particularly with this practice) with the processing if you write about what you experienced.

## Week 6-The Last Time

### Inspirational Reading:

Reflecting on my life, I realize there were pivotal moments that marked the last time I engaged in certain activities that I so loved. As a child or teenager, we often don't comprehend the significance of these "lasts." One memorable instance for me was the final football game of my senior year in high school. As I left the field, tears streaming down my face, I knew I would never wear those cleats or pads or play the game I loved so dearly again.

There are countless last moments in adulthood, too. Fully understanding and appreciating the transient nature of these moments can lead us to be truly present because any could be our last. A particularly poignant example from my life was the unexpected loss of my beloved mother. A force of nature into her mid-80s, she was an ardent gym-goer, up at 5:30 am every day, walking her mile around the indoor track or doing swim aerobics with her friends. Her sudden passing after a minor hernia surgery left me devastated. The thought of her rapid passing still takes my breath away as she and I spoke weekly; she was my biggest fan and encourager.

Throughout the year, I often find myself reflecting on our shared experiences, wishing I'd known they were to be our last. A standout memory is our shared Christmas morning tradition of cooking breakfast for the family. Mom would make her famous biscuits, eggs, country ham, grits, and bacon while I made the Chilton family's famous sausage gravy. This recipe had been passed down to me from my father, who had died from cancer at age 66.

How I wish that I had known that last Christmas breakfast would be the final one we would cook together. Somehow, I would have found a way to be more present and take it all in. I would have stayed in the kitchen, soaked in her presence, and had another cup of coffee with her as our large family was putting all the gifts under the tree. If I had known that it would be our last time, I would have found a way to hold on to her a little longer, sit next to her as we opened gifts, and insisted that she stay just a bit longer on this beautiful Christmas Day. But we don't know, do we?

I believe the key to avoiding regrets is treating each moment as if it were our last, particularly those moments with our loved ones. This practice requires a tranquil and thoughtful contemplation of the present and the people we are with.

Take an everyday scene, like your spouse or partner engrossed in a book. Truly notice them, absorb every detail as if it were your last time seeing them. In reality, this will be the last time you will ever see them in this particular moment. Do this with your friends. Really pay attention to what they're saying without thinking about what you will say back as if it is the last time you will ever hear them.

I promise you that if you do this, you will elevate your life to a much higher plane as you live each day in the present moment with the people you love. This practice has not only taught me that this moment is all we truly have, but it's also taught me a lot about gratitude for these moments, these experiences, and for life itself.

This exercise is not meant to be morbid, nor an invitation to fear or panic about the potential loss of a loved one. There's no room for such emotions here. Instead, it provides the path towards gratitude, contentment, and the chance to live an abundant, full life by being present in the moment… every single moment.

Each moment is filled with life, unique and unrepeatable. As you cultivate mindfulness with your loved ones, you will likely incorporate this practice into your daily activities. Imagine all the new joy and appreciation this simple practice will bring to your life.

**Meditation and Mindfulness Practice:**

I love country music, and one of my all-time favorite songs is the 2007 Diamond Rio hit, "One More Day." It speaks of losing someone very special and desperately wanting just one more day. Honestly, I cry almost every time I hear the song. I want you to find it (Google, Apple

Music, Spotify, or wherever you listen to music) and listen to it to get into the mood.

Some of the lyrics are,

*Last night I had a crazy dream*
*A wish was granted just for me*
*It could be for anything*
*I didn't ask for money*
*Or a mansion in Malibu*
*I simply wished for one more day with you*

*First thing I'd do is pray for time to crawl*
*I'd unplug the telephone and keep the TV off*
*I'd hold you every second*
*Say a million I love you's*
*That's what I'd do with one more day with you.*

In this week's meditation exercise, I would like you to begin by finding a peaceful spot where you won't be disturbed. Sit comfortably, close your eyes, and take a few deep breaths. Inhale and exhale slowly, feeling your chest rise and fall with each breath.

Now, start to recall your day yesterday, from the moment you woke up to the moment you went to bed. Take your time to recall as many details as you can. If making a list works better, take out a sheet of paper, open your eyes, and start documenting. What was the first thing you did when you woke up? What was your morning routine? What did you eat for breakfast? How did your day unfold?

Now, move on to the people you interacted with. Who were they? What conversations did you have? What decisions did you make? Try to recollect as much as possible. Think about the time you spent on various activities such as work, hobbies, and even social media. Overall, how did you feel? Were there moments of stress, joy, worry, or boredom? Let these memories surface without judgment.

Now, imagine that yesterday was your last day alive on earth. Everything you just listed was the last things you said or did. How would your actions change if you knew it was your last day? What would you choose to do differently? What would you say, and to whom? What would you eat? How would you express love, gratitude, or forgiveness? Would you have spent your time differently? Would you have treated yourself or others differently?

Sit with these thoughts and allow feelings and emotions to come up. There is no right or wrong answer, only what feels true. This exercise is a reminder of the impermanence of life and the value of living each day as if it were your last. It's not meant to induce fear but to inspire mindfulness and purpose in how we live our lives.

When you're ready, bring your attention back to your breath. Take a few more deep breaths, and when you feel ready, slowly open your eyes.

I know I am describing only one mindfulness exercise for this week, so it would be wonderful if you think about it and let it absorb into your fabric all through the week. Think about and try out all the ways you would live if you knew this day would be your last.

All of us must learn, as underscored by Tim McGraw's powerful 2004 chart-topper, to "live like you were dying." Notice the change in how you feel and treat others. Also, observe how others feel and act around you. *This one exercise may just change your life.*

**Self-Reflection:** How did this exercise make you feel? On your "last day," what did you do the same, and what did you do differently? If you practiced this often, do you think it would change the way you live and the quality of your life?

# Step 3 –

# The Art of Surrender

## Week 7-What We Resist Persists

**Inspirational Reading:**

"The only way out is through." This oft-repeated saying encapsulates a truth that Swiss psychologist Carl Jung echoed in his famous quote, "What you resist not only persists, but will grow in size." There are similar variants of this wisdom - "You always get what you resist," for instance. The essence of these observations is that life, at some point, will present us with unexpected and often unwelcome challenges.

For someone like me, who has a complex job managing around 25 direct reports, unexpected issues arise several times a week. However, life also presents us with significantly more devastating experiences, such as the loss of our health, the breakdown of a marriage, sudden unemployment, or the death of a loved one.

Reacting to these major losses and disappointments with grief is a natural human response. Yet, some of us become entangled in a cycle of suffering, magnifying the unfairness of our predicament and replaying scenarios of how we might have averted such events. These tendencies lock us in the past and thereby extend our suffering, sometimes indefinitely. We get caught in the trap of thinking, "This is so unfair. It shouldn't be this way. I don't want this. If only I had done this or that differently."

By resisting the reality of our circumstances, we unwittingly prolong our pain. In our futile attempt to control or change the past - a complete impossibility - we fight reality by clinging to an illusion of what could have been. This struggle leads us adrift in an endless sea of "Why Me?"

Jung's insight is both simple and extraordinarily challenging to put into practice. It requires us to surrender control, to accept life's inevitable pain, struggles, and unwanted events. In Chapter 7, I discuss the concepts of Impermanence and the "Law of Undulation" and how they refer to the natural ebb and flow of human emotions, spirituality, and events. Both describe how ups and downs, triumphs, and devastations are a natural part of the human experience.

However, C. S. Lewis took this concept a step further; he believed it was the difficult times, not the good times, that God most used to draw individuals into relationships. Lewis believed that God uses the "tough" periods of loss and spiritual dryness not as a punishment but as a tool for spiritual growth[15]. This was certainly echoed by Josh's story in Chapter 7.

However, I must emphasize that acceptance and surrender aren't equivalent to giving up on life. It isn't an admission of defeat but a commitment to reality. I believe the act of acceptance and letting go accomplishes four significant things:

First, it acknowledges the reality of our circumstances, summed up in the pragmatic phrase, "It is what it is." Resistance to reality is like fighting quicksand; the more you struggle, the deeper you sink. From a neurological perspective, the more we engage the neural circuits responsible for resisting and ruminating about the past, the stronger these circuits become. This ultimately entraps us in a victim mindset, a dangerous mental state that only deepens our suffering. Take one step too far toward victimhood, and it is impossible to return.

Second, acceptance reminds us that the present is the only moment we can influence. We can't alter the past or control the future, but we have the power to shape the present moment into something beautiful.

Third, acceptance allows us to confront our most painful and frightening emotions head-on, particularly through practices like meditation. I lost my beloved mother and had a devastating horse accident in a very short period of time. Meditation was vitally important for me, particularly in the face of these personal tragedies. Each day, I was reminded that there is a place of peace where I can encounter my deepest fears and sorrows, surrender them to a higher power and experience a significant reduction in their capacity to hurt me. This was also where I sensed the spirit of my mom most strongly.

This reminds me of the second step of Alcoholics Anonymous 12-Step Program: I "came to believe that a Power greater than ourselves could restore us to sanity." This step invites members to accept that they aren't alone in the struggle with their recovery and there is a higher power, however they choose to define it, that can assist in restoring their sanity and overcoming their addiction. This higher power doesn't necessarily have to be religious or spiritual but can also represent the group's collective power.

Finally, acceptance opens the door to creativity. When we stop struggling against the past, we free up mental resources that we can use to construct a brighter future. Once we step out of the mire of resistance, we can start building a new, positive path forward.

So, while the phrase "what we resist, persists" might initially sound like a harsh truth during the worst of life's experiences, it also carries a promise of liberation. We can only open a path to a more fulfilling future when we stop wrestling with the past and start accepting the present.

**Meditation and Mindfulness Practice:**

Begin by finding a quiet, comfortable space where you can sit undisturbed. Settle into a comfortable position and close your eyes. Start with a few deep breaths to help you relax and focus your mind. Inhale deeply through your nose, hold for a moment, then exhale slowly through your mouth. Do this for a few cycles until you feel centered and calm.

For meditations during week 7, I want you to consider some things you've been resisting. It could be feelings, thoughts, situations, or a person/people. Try to visualize these as vividly as you can each day, as if it were right in front of you.

As you hold the image in your mind each day, allow yourself to fully acknowledge it. Instead of pushing it away or trying to change it, simply observe it. Recognize that your resistance to it might give it much more power and energy than it actually has. Realize that this resistance likely causes it to persist and grow larger.

Instead of resisting, allow yourself to be curious about this thing. Ask yourself why am I resisting this? What does this say about me? Are there emotions it brings up? What can I learn from it? Try to be as open and non-judgmental as possible in this exploration.

As you explore, you might start to feel uncomfortable emotions. Instead of resisting these feelings, try to welcome them as well. Label each emotion as it arises and accept it as a part of your meditation experience. It can't hurt you in this form. You are in a safe space.

Throughout this exercise, gently bring your mind back to the object of your resistance and your breath if your mind starts to wander. Remember, the goal is not to rid yourself of this thing or situation you resist but to observe it, understand it, weaken it, and thereby react to it better.

Practice this for 10-15 minutes or for however long feels comfortable for you.

To finish, take a few more deep breaths, then gently open your eyes. Take a moment to acknowledge the work you've done. Remember, you might not have solved the issue, but you've taken a significant step toward understanding it and reducing its power over you.

This can be a difficult week that will take courage. However, each practice will help you develop the capacity to face and explore what you resist day to day. It will allow you to learn from these experiences rather than allowing them to control you. Over time, this practice will help to diminish the size and influence these issues have over your life.

**Self-Reflection:** How did this practice make you feel? What have you been resisting? What in your life has greater power than it should because of resistance?

## Week 8-The Incredible Power of Observing

### Inspirational Reading:

In the fogginess of our consciousness, there exist fears we avoid, emotions we suppress, and thoughts we refuse to acknowledge. These hidden elements surface when we meditate, often making us more anxious. But this is not a sign of failure or vulnerability. On the contrary, it is evidence that our minds are undergoing transformation, that we are becoming aware of what we've been unknowingly clinging to.

The next step of this journey invites a profound metaphysical question. Last week, I asked you to observe what you have resisted and how it will weaken. Do you think you can simply observe your internal experiences as a detached witness and change your relationship with these thoughts and emotions? What happens when we sense anxiety creeping in and choose not to engage with it?

This concept, known as the observer effect, first emerged as the result of a strange quantum physics experiment. Groundbreaking experiments in the 1920s demonstrated that the mere act of observing a quantum phenomenon alters its behavior. Particles such as electrons behave differently depending on whether they are being observed. Even more puzzling, later studies suggested that these particles seemed to "know" if we intend to observe them.

For reductionist scientists, this concept was deeply unsettling. If reality changes based on our observation, what does "reality" truly mean? Translated into the realm of mindfulness, can the mere act of observing our thoughts and emotions, without engaging with them, alter these experiences, or at least our relationship to them? If we refrain from fueling the flames of our feelings, do they intensify or diminish?

Recent research provides reassurance that the flames indeed die down. The simple act of observing, without engagement, can significantly reduce the power of our negative unconscious emotions and thoughts. This understanding offers a powerful tool for overcoming the detrimental effects of these experiences.

I recall a personal experience from my middle school years that perfectly illustrates this. I used to be the target of a bully who routinely insulted and even physically hit me. I lived in constant fear, dreading what he might do to me next. My fear amplified his strength, making him appear an insurmountable monster.

One day, I decided I had had enough. I turned around and faced my tormentor, maintaining a steady gaze. I didn't fight back or shout insults. I simply looked at him intensely. Over the following weeks, his influence over me faded. The fear of him had been far more traumatizing than any physical altercation we might have had. Even had he chosen to hit me, the physical pain could not have matched the emotional distress I had put myself through in anticipation.

More recently, after my devastating horse accident, I sat in meditation, sometimes for hours each day, to face my most frightening thoughts, emotions, and pain. I was convinced that if I ever recovered from this accident, I would never ride a horse, much less a 'hot' Arabian horse again. However, the more time I spent in meditation facing my fears and pain, the stronger I became, including my anxiety about getting on a horse again. On the one-year anniversary of my accident, I got back on the horse (not the same horse that bucked me off, but another Arabian) for a 10-mile trail ride. Was I still a bit frightened? Yes! But I did it anyway. I strongly believe we must face our fears, and my year of observing in meditation allowed me to do just that.

All of this demonstrates how our fear-based emotions can create unnecessary suffering. The primitive parts of our brains, such as the amygdala and the limbic system, are wired to fear potential threats, a useful trait in dangerous ancestral environments but less applicable in our modern world. Thus, when we encounter these fear-based thoughts and feelings, we can simply observe them with curiosity, courage, and even humor. When we do so, they lose their power over us.

In this way, the observer effect becomes a source of liberation from our deepest fears, showing us that observing can transform our relationship with our fears. Instead of allowing our fears to consume us, we can face them, observe them, and thereby reduce their hold on us. In the light of observation, the frightening aspects of fear start to fade.

**Meditation and Mindfulness Practice:**

Start by finding a comfortable position, sitting or lying, in a quiet, distraction-free space. Close your eyes and take a few deep breaths. Inhale deeply through your nose, hold it for a moment, then slowly exhale through your mouth. Feel your body relaxing with each breath.

Once you feel settled, shift your focus to the act of observation. Begin with your body. Notice the sensation of your clothes against your skin, the feeling of the chair or floor beneath you, the temperature of the room, even any pain you may be feeling. Observe these sensations without trying to change or judge them. Just notice and accept them as they are.

Next, move your attention to your thoughts. Let them come and go without trying to hold onto them or push them away. Observe each thought as it arises, and let it pass like a cloud floating across the sky. You're not these thoughts; you're just observing them. Remember, each of these thoughts is auditioning for your attention. Don't give them that power. Just let them float by.

Now, turn your focus to your emotions. Maybe you're feeling calm, or perhaps there's a hint of anxiety or restlessness. Whatever emotions arise, observe them without judgment or attachment, name them just as they are. Recognize that emotions, like thoughts, are temporary and changing. If you don't engage with them, they will lessen and eventually move from your mind.

As your awareness deepens, see if you can observe the Observer (be patient, this can take months or even years). This might feel a bit tricky, but the idea is for you to become aware of your own awareness, your *I*, your true *Self*. With this move, you notice the part of you that's noticing. This, in turn, can help you tap into a deeper sense of presence and consciousness.

For the final minute, bring your observation back to your breath. Notice the rise and fall of your chest, the feeling of the air entering and exiting your nostrils. As you end your meditation, take one more deep breath, then slowly open your eyes, bringing your mindfulness and this sense of observation into the rest of your day.

Remember, meditation and observation are skills that take practice. Be patient and take this time to observe and be present. In particular, don't get discouraged if you are unable to become aware of your awareness in just a week. This took years and a devastating horse accident before I began to understand the nature of my awareness.

**Self-Reflection:** What thoughts, emotions and/or physical pain did you observe? Were you able to just watch them and allow them to lessen?

## Week 9-Letting Go of the Unthinkable

### Inspirational Reading:

Surrender is not a concept that has come easily to me. I have spent most of my lifetime believing I could do or overcome almost anything if I tried hard enough. Consequently, for so long, surrender seemed to represent everything I opposed in how I lived my life.  Surrender has several definitions, including "to cease resistance to an enemy or opponent", "to give up", "to hand over" or "to raise the white flag."

I first began to understand the power of surrender while attending 12-Step Family Support meetings during my son Josh's eight-year battle with an opiate addiction. As you have learned from Chapter 7, Josh was a star football player for a large high school when a car accident left him paralyzed from the waist down. After several surgeries, he became addicted to opiate painkillers. The addiction slowly overtook my son's life right at the time when the United States began to see a dramatic increase in opioid (Fentanyl) overdose-related deaths in 2014. Josh lived with me for part of the time. When he didn't, he was often homeless in the streets. I will never forget a visit with a counselor in 2016. This professional told me that Josh was on the verge of dying from an overdose, so "get prepared."

I accepted his suggestion to attend 12-Step Family Support meetings. For at least three days a week for several months, I sat silently in the meetings, devastated by my helplessness. I could not stop the unimaginable. My son's downward spiral seemed to lead inevitably to his untimely death. I tried surrendering to my powerlessness over the situation but kept attempting to regain control. Although letting go wasn't a perfect process, eventually, it became easier, and my life, and oddly enough, Josh's life, became much calmer. As I learned to surrender, I stopped enabling Josh and allowed him the emotional space to recover on his own terms.

As I discussed in detail in Chapter 7, we must accept and live by what C.S. Lewis called the "Law of Undulation"[15]. This means that the only constant thing is change. Thus, our lives, situations, health, relationships, and passions are always in flux. Unfortunately, change brings about natural responses like confusion, fear, and discouragement. This growing momentum of thoughts can drown us in a tidal wave of negative feelings and adverse reactions. By expecting undulation as a normal part of life, we can begin to see the value of daily surrender.

My experience with Josh and the thought of his loss was unthinkable at the time, but it also taught me that resisting the "is-ness" of the now only results in more distress for ourselves and those we love. There is an incredible power in surrendering and letting go of those difficult situations and associated feelings we can't control. Through surrender, we can find relief from the agony of our difficult pasts and current stressful situations. In fact, I have learned that the daily practice of surrender is vital for me to continue to find joy, freedom, and physical and emotional well-being and allow the happiness within me to emerge.

**Meditation and Mindfulness Practice:**

In this week's mindfulness practice, I want to begin by rereading Reverend Safire Rose's poem from Chapter 8. I have placed it here again.

If possible, print the poem out. It's okay if you don't, but I want you to consider what you need to let go of. In lines 1-7 and lines 10-13, Safire lists the things she let go of. I want you to spend time this week listing the situations, fears, and emotions you need to let go of. Write them down in your journal.

*She let go.*

*Without a thought or a word, she let go.*

*She let go of fear. She let go of the judgments.*
*She let go of the confluence of opinions swarming around her head.*
*She let go of the committee of indecision within her.*
*She let go of all the 'right' reasons. Wholly and completely,*
*without hesitation or worry, she just let go.*

*She didn't ask anyone for advice. She didn't read a book on how to let go... She didn't search the scriptures.*

*She just let go.*
*She let go of all of the memories that held her back.*
*She let go of all of the anxiety that kept her from moving forward.*
*She let go of the planning and all of the calculations about how to do it just right.*

*She didn't promise to let go.*
*She didn't journal about it.*
*She didn't write the projected date in her day-timer.*
*She made no public announcement and put no ad in the paper.*
*She didn't check the weather report or read her daily horoscope.*

*She just let go.*
*She didn't analyze whether she should let go.*
*She didn't call her friends to discuss the matter.*
*She didn't do a five-step Spiritual Mind Treatment.*
*She didn't call the prayer line.*
*She didn't utter one word. She just let go.*

*No one was around when it happened.*
*There was no applause or congratulations.*
*No one thanked her or praised her.*
*No one noticed a thing.*

*Like a leaf falling from a tree, she just let go.*
*There was no effort. There was no struggle.*
*It wasn't good and it wasn't bad.*
*It was what it was, and it is just that.*
*In the space of letting go, she let it all be.*
*A small smile came over her face.*
*A light breeze blew through her.*
*And the sun and the moon shone forevermore.*

— Reverend Safire Rose

At the end of your journaling with your list in hand, I want you to let go of something on that list with the following 5-minute meditation. A close friend of mine inspired this meditation. She had this vision several times while going through a highly destructive divorce that was pulling her family apart.

Begin by finding a quiet, comfortable space to sit or lie down. Take a few deep breaths, inhaling slowly and then exhaling even slower. Close your eyes and picture sitting on the edge of a rapidly moving stream. In your hands, you hold a rough rope that extends into the water, attached to a boat tugged by the current. The rope is coarse, and your grip is so tight it's making your hands raw and bloody.

Now, in the boat, visualize the thing you find hard to let go of. It could be a past mistake, a painful memory, a lost relationship, or any burden that you've listed. Feel the tension in your hands as you grip that rope. Notice the discomfort, the pain. Be aware of how much energy it takes to hold on and resist the pull of the stream.

Now, slowly start to loosen your grip on the rope. Feel immediate relief as you do so, yet at the same time, the fear of what you may be losing. This is normal. It's okay to be scared. This is part of letting go.

And then, when you're ready, release your hold completely. Let the rope slip from your hands. See the blood slowly wash away. Feel the pain subsiding. Watch as the boat is carried away by the stream, growing smaller and smaller in the distance until it's out of sight. It's gone, but you're still here, stronger for having released it.

Take a few moments to feel the peace that comes with letting go. Acknowledge the space you've created for new experiences and emotions to enter. Remember, letting go doesn't mean forgetting or minimizing. It simply means you've chosen not to let it hold power over you anymore. Breathe into that newfound freedom.

When you're ready, slowly open your eyes and return to your surroundings with a new feeling of release, freedom, and peace.

**Self-Reflection:** What did you let go of? What touched you about this meditation? Did you feel lighter after it?

# Step 4 -

# Trust the Journey

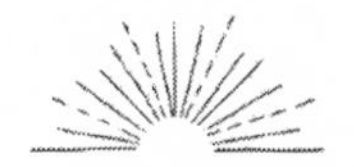

## Week 10-Becoming a Child, Again

**Inspirational Reading:**

When I look into a child's eyes or watch them play, the characteristic that the child has that most of us have lost is innocence. In their purest form, a child cannot lie, masquerade, manipulate, or pretend to be anything other than what they are. This sense of authenticity is seen throughout nature. A dog is just a dog, a rose is a rose, and a star is a star. Everything simply is what it is, even without giving it a name. Its beauty has not been altered in any way.

As adults, we lose this innocence. We learn to present ourselves as something different than our true *Selves*. Perhaps our most egregious sin as parents is tapping down our children's honesty, innocence, and beauty. When children are scolded for expressing their honest thoughts and emotions, they learn it is necessary to hide their true *Selves*. They, in turn, begin to lose that innocence and are moved into the adult world of illusions. This ultimately results in identity confusion as the child begins to hide the truth from others and themselves. We forget how to be a child.

I now would ask you to reflect on how much of your childhood innocence you believe you still have. Do you have people around you who let you be yourself, as transparent, honest, and naive as a child?

The loss of childhood innocence also occurs in more subtle ways. For instance, when children are taught to aspire to be someone else. We often encourage our children to be successful, famous, powerful, and not necessarily what they innately are drawn to. They may want to be musicians, cooks, artists, gardeners, or inventors, but they are pushed to strive to be 'somebody.' Eventually, this lack of resonance will lead to unhappiness.

So, for most of us, with time, our innocence and beauty fades when we opt for self-promotion over self-expression. I urge you, in as many ways as possible, to surrender to your nature and become what you were meant to be. For at least a significant portion of everyday become what you think you should be. I typically walk across campus every day, lay under a tree, and just observe. Looking up, my eyes meet a beautiful lattice of branches spreading out in all directions, creating a vast, intricate network. The leaves rustle gently in the breeze, creating a soothing, whispering sound that resonates deep within me. I feel the life of the tree around me. From the tiny insects that call it home to the birds that flit from branch to branch, their delicate songs fill the air. All this makes me feel connected to a life far grander and older than myself. Perhaps you feel something similar playing with your child or your dog.

I have a favorite tee shirt that reads, "Stay Wild." For a long while, I couldn't understand why I was so innately attracted to this saying. Now I understand that this calls me back to nature, to the wildness of childhood, and away from "what I think I 'should' be." Adults who maintain their innocence and wildness do so by remaining untainted, allowing innocence and nature's path to guide them without any ulterior motive to impress others.

Preserving innocence is a journey of surrender with a constant awareness of one's internal and external world. This heightened awareness brings us into the present moment and stillness and protects us from the pressures of society and 'adult' realities. Surrendering our 'adult' realities and inviting in innocence and gratitude will transform us. Welcome back your sense of childhood wonder.

Think about the fear that imprisons your unique spark of originality. This is a fear of ridicule or rejection if you dare to be yourself and refuse to conform in how you dress, act, think, react, feel, and uphold your values. Sadly, by succumbing to these societal norms, we find ourselves in a realm dominated by the manipulative and domineering, losing childhood innocence in the process. We destroy our innocence when we let go of simplicity when we let comparison, competition, and the pursuit of hollow achievements be our driving factor. This moves us away from a blissful state of being and into the darkness inhabited by most adults. The courage to step away from this conformity allows us to reclaim our original innocence.

It is time to revolt against this adult state of existence. It is time to liberate yourself from the chains that bind you. Doing so will let you reclaim the kingdom of innocence and wildness where children abide.

**Meditation and Mindfulness Practice:**

This is fun week! This week, we allow nature to absorb us into her and to nurture and bring us back to our inner child. When we talk about 'becoming a child again' as I did in Chapter 10, we're really speaking to recapturing a sense of unbridled wonder, innocence, and the ability to be present and fascinated by nature's magical, mystical stillness. In its raw and magnificent glory, I believe nature offers us a powerful way to rekindle childlike qualities that we may have lost decades ago.

Every weekend, I take a 4-mile hike into the Catalina Mountain range near Tucson, AZ, and become absorbed by the sky, cacti, plant, and animal life that this magnificent mountain range provides. As I step out, refreshed from the mountains each week, a new man, or should I say a new child, emerges. I always do the same routine. I walk to the highest point at the base of a geological formation called Cathedral Rock. I have a special spot where I can observe, hear, smell, taste, and become aware of everything.

This week, I am going to give you two exercises connecting nature to your inner child. First, find a place in nature where you feel comfortable and safe. It could be a local park, a small patch of woods, a beach, a mountain trail, or even your own backyard or garden. The key is finding a place to be quiet and undisturbed. Start by taking a slow, leisurely walk. Pay attention to how the earth feels under your feet. Take note of the different sounds you hear - birds chirping, leaves rustling, water flowing. Allow these sensations to ground you in the present moment.

Then, find a place to sit or lie down for 10-15minutes. Begin this time with any of the mindfulness exercises we've previously explored. For example, choose your breath as the focal point of your awareness, but keep your eyes open this time. Notice not only the easily perceived sights and sensations but also the subtler ones. Try, if possible, to refrain from labeling what you see, only sense and feel. Remember, very young children typically don't know the names of things. Just observe and fully experience them without attaching labels. Again, move through all the senses, including sounds, smells, and tastes.

Walking back, I always find something in nature that I can deeply connect with. It may be a cactus, tree, group of birds, or insects. For example, there may be a tree that calls you to it. Spend some time observing the tree. Notice its height, the spread of its branches, the color and texture of its leaves, and the sunshine emerging through the leaves. Look at the shape and depth of its roots and take the time to touch the bark of the tree. Feel its texture. Is it rough or smooth, dry or moist? Lean against the tree and close your eyes. Feel the strength and stability of its trunk. Place your hands on the bark and sense the life within and how it provides that life and inner child back to you. You can do this with anything you see in nature. Nature has been waiting hundreds of millions of years to give back to you.

Feel the connection you've forged with nature and the childlike joy from this simple, mindful engagement. Remember, this exercise isn't about achieving anything. It's about reconnecting with your inner child and rekindling a sense of curiosity, playfulness, and awe. And most importantly, it is about having fun!

**Self-Reflection:** What surprised you about your mindful trip into nature? Did you begin to connect with your inner child? What inspired you most?

## Week 11-The Guest House

**Inspirational Reading:**

When I began meditating six years ago, I had no idea what I was doing or where my spiritual journey would lead me. As an achievement-obsessed Westerner, I would have been much more comfortable with a plan and a set of goals. However, I now realize that projecting potential future outcomes would have countered everything I have learned about this mystic journey. I now know this journey cannot be written down as a set of simple do's and don't's in a self-help book.

I want to be honest with you. Even at this point in my journey, there are times when it is not always easy. No matter how experienced you are, it will be difficult to address the onslaught of chatter, insecurities, and problems arising from your unconscious mind and the external world. For most of us, the path to awareness is gradual. Even now, at least once a month, I find myself back in the swamp, reacting to a situation as if I have never seen a meditation cushion. But here's the difference: within 24 hours, I realize that I allowed myself to enter the swamp and consequently must be resisting something in my life that will take me to the next level of deep transformation.

During the past few years, the 13th century mystic poet Rumi has fundamentally impacted my view of life. In perhaps his most well-known poem, "The Guest House," he compares being human to a guest house with new arrivals of struggles every morning. In the poem, he reminds us not to resist painful thoughts, problems, disappointments, and difficult people but to meet them all honorably with courage, joy, and respect.

*This being human is a guest house.*

*Every morning a new arrival.*

*A joy, a depression, a meanness,*

*some momentary awareness comes*

*as an unexpected visitor.*

*Welcome and entertain them all!*

*Even if they're a crowd of sorrows,*

*who violently sweep your house*

*empty of its furniture,*

*still, treat each guest honorably.*

*He may be clearing you out*

*for some new delight.*

*The dark thought, the shame, the malice,*

*meet them at the door laughing,*

*and invite them in.*

*Be grateful for whoever comes,*

*because each has been sent*

*as a guide from beyond.*

Jalaluddin Rumi, as translated by Coleman Barks

This magnificent poem by Rumi serves as a poignant reminder, urging us not only to embrace but to appreciate our troubles, for they are "sent as a guide from beyond." You now realize that several preceding meditations have revolved around shedding the aspects of our past conditioning and present struggles that sow suffering. I intentionally presented these perspectives from various angles; for a significant portion of our spiritual expedition involves liberating ourselves from the clutches of our history and basking in the freedom of the present.

In life, we will encounter many "guests" that we would love to resist or at least ignore. However, if we truly believe that these are being sent to deepen the evolution of our consciousness, we must find a place of stillness that allows us to accept the "is-ness" of our situations. Our journey is not about changing others or avoiding the difficulties that arise in our lives. It is about changing us and how we respond to life.

I believe ascending levels of consciousness cannot be achieved by utilizing typical Western counseling approaches that focus on the "whys" behind dysfunctional behaviors. Believe me, I have tried. I often joke with folks that I have spent enough money on counseling to build several counseling centers. I still go to weekly counseling with a wonderful therapist. These sessions provide great insight into the sources of emotional problems. However, a better understanding of the difficulty has not been enough for me to 'correct' my problems. In fact, in some cases, I believe by focusing on the causes of destructive emotions, we may, in fact, provide momentum to the very thoughts strengthening them.

It took me decades to grasp Rumi's central message in "The Guest House." Resisting painful feelings will, in fact, block my progress. Instead, experiencing and then letting go of pain and unwanted feelings often provides the sought-after liberation from emotional addictions and the damage they cause. I don't know exactly how or why this letting go is so effective or how it has made me calmer and softer, but I am okay with that. I have come to view enlightenment as a direction we aim at and not a destination to be reached or a "why" to be answered.

**Meditation and Mindfulness Practice:**

Find a quiet place where you will be undisturbed for the duration of 15-20 minutes. Sit comfortably and close your eyes. Begin by taking a few deep breaths, inhaling through your nose, and exhaling through your mouth. With each exhale, allow yourself to let go of any tension you might be holding.

Now, recall the words of Rumi's "The Guest House". Better yet, if you have a copy of the poem, read it out loud before beginning this exercise. Remind yourself that each moment, feeling, and thought is like a visitor to the house of your consciousness.

With this imagery in mind, turn your attention to the 'guests' currently in your 'house.' Instead of trying to change or judge the guests, simply observe them. There might be emotions, sensations, or thoughts present, but remind yourself that all guests are invited to stay for a while.

As each 'guest' comes into your awareness, acknowledge it. If it's a thought, simply label it 'thinking'. If it's an emotion, name the emotion: 'joy', 'sadness', 'anger', or 'contentment.' If it's a physical sensation, label it as 'sensation.' Treat each guest with equal respect and curiosity, whether it's a sensation of peace, a pang of sorrow, or a nagging worry. Invite them in as Rumi encourages us to do.

Remember, some guests may be pleasant, others very unpleasant. Each one has something important to teach you. Don't resist them. Meet them at the door smiling and invite them in. Be grateful for whoever comes because each has been sent as a guide.

Remember that our very existence here is an incredible gift, but this gift comes with incredible blessings and suffering, and we often learn more from difficult situations. Practice this for 10-15 minutes or for however long it feels comfortable for you. If your mind wanders or becomes overwhelmed, gently bring it back to the breath.

To finish the exercise, take a few more deep breaths, then gently open your eyes. Take a moment to appreciate the diversity of 'guests' that visited your 'house' and the lessons they brought or are bringing you.

**Self-Reflection:** What/who were your guests? Were you able to welcome each one? What do you think you are learning from each one?

## Week 12-Choose Forgiveness

### Inspirational Reading:

I've endeavored to provide an authentic reflection of my spiritual journey over the past six decades in this book. This has been a journey encompassing all shades of experiences: the pleasant, the painful, the fearful, the challenging, and the disheartening. My current perspective enables me to see my narrative differently. I now appreciate that there were no genuinely bad or ugly experiences. Each event, each decision, has woven a thread into the intricate tapestry of my life, resulting in a unique and beautiful portrayal of my existence. Admittedly, I've caused pain to others and myself. I have often fallen short of love and kindness due to my limited understanding of the profound influence my unconscious mind exerted over my choices and reactions.

As you know by now, I deeply revere the life and teachings of Jesus. One of Jesus's final utterances before His agonizing death on the cross profoundly moves me. He pleads, "Father, forgive them, for they do not know what they are doing." Until a few years ago, I interpreted this plea as addressing those directly responsible for His crucifixion: the Romans and the Pharisees. However, I now believe that His words were meant for us all, the entire collective navigating this human condition. We must learn to forgive and love others and ourselves, recognizing that for much of our lives, we stumble in darkness, largely unaware of our actions and their consequences. Love, forgiveness, and compassion are the fruits of waking up and living a spiritual life.

Over time, I have recognized the truth in Eckhart Tolle's assertion that "Being spiritual has nothing to do with what you believe and everything to do with your state of consciousness." With these words, I wish to encourage you, the reader, to have faith in your journey and acknowledge its spiritual nature. This journey will guide you to your authentic *Self*, your *I*, and the Divine residing within you and all around. This realization will provide you with a limitless resource of love and enable you to extend a healing touch, companionship, and compassion to everyone you encounter, including yourself.

**Meditation and Mindfulness Practice:**

One of the profound spiritual insights I've gained, particularly relevant to the process of forgiveness, is the understanding that at any given moment, our actions reflect our consciousness (or unconsciousness) level. The acts of others that might have caused us pain or distress are typically a mirror of their own state of consciousness at that time. It's crucial to realize that had you been in their shoes, possessing their unconsciousness level, your actions would likely have mirrored theirs without your spiritual journey toward awareness. This doesn't necessarily mean that we let toxic people back into our lives and continue to harm us. It simply provides a deeper level of understanding of their actions.

Similarly, when we reflect on our past deeds that we might now find unforgivable, we must recognize that we acted according to the level of unconsciousness we possessed at that time. In both cases, this perspective fosters compassion and enables forgiveness toward others and us. Through the lens of compassion and forgiveness, love can reemerge.

The last meditation is designed to enhance this important understanding. I anticipate the first part of this exercise lasting 5-10 minutes. Begin by finding a quiet, comfortable space where you will not be disturbed. Take a seat in a relaxed position, close your eyes, and begin to notice your breath. Take a few deep breaths, inhaling deeply through your nose and exhaling slowly through your mouth. Let the exhale be longer than the inhale, letting your body feel a sense of relaxation and release.

Bring to mind someone who has hurt you or caused you great distress. Visualize them in front of you. Now, try to view this person from their level of higher consciousness. Remember (in Chapter 4), David Hawkins constructed a scale for different levels of consciousness, ranging from one to 1000, and suggested that the level of courage, at 200, marks the critical shift from negative to positive consciousness levels. Importantly, he also pointed out that consciousness levels below 200 are destructive to the individual and those around them, while levels above strengthen both the individual and others[12].

Recognize that we and others act from our level of consciousness at the time, influenced by our own experiences, fears, and perceptions. This does not excuse their or our actions but allows for understanding and forgiveness. Again, proper boundaries and actions often must be put in place to protect us from highly destructive people, but these actions can now be done from the perspective of compassion.

Hold this understanding and say to them in your mind, "I acknowledge your level of consciousness at that time. I forgive you." It is also okay if you are not yet ready for this step. Visualize this space as sacred with a warm light radiating from you to them. If you are not ready to do this, envision the warm light emanating from the Divine who can help you forgive in time.

Stay in this space for a while, noticing any emotions or thoughts that come up. If any negative feelings arise, gently acknowledge them and return to meditation.

Now, for the next 5-10 minutes, we will transition from someone else to you. Take a few deep breaths again. As you breathe in, visualize peace and forgiveness filling your body. As you breathe out, imagine letting go of past hurts.

Now, think about a past action of your own that you find difficult to forgive. Try to see this past self from your current higher level of consciousness. Acknowledge that you were acting from the only level of consciousness available to you at the time.

Hold compassion for your past self, recognizing the limitations of your consciousness at that time. In your mind, say: "I acknowledge my mistake but realize why I did it, and I forgive myself." Visualize this forgiveness as a soothing light enveloping you.

Remain in this space for a while, aware of any feelings or thoughts. If difficult emotions emerge, acknowledge them and gently bring your attention back to self-forgiveness. Finally, take a few more deep breaths, imagining each breath bringing in love and compassion and releasing any lingering self-judgment or guilt. Gradually, bring your attention back to your surroundings. Open your eyes slowly when you are ready. Place your arms around yourself, one arm over the other, and hug yourself. Stay here as long as you need to. You are loved, and you are worthy of love.

**Self-Reflection:** How did this meditation make you feel? Were you able to feel love and compassion for others? Yourself?

## Week 13 Conclusion-What Is It You Plan to Do with Your One Wild and Precious Life?

### Inspirational Reading:

Please read Mary Oliver's poem, "The Summer Day"

*Who made the world?*

*Who made the swan, and the black bear?*

*Who made the grasshopper?*

*This grasshopper, I mean--*

*the one who has flung herself out of the grass,*

*the one who is eating sugar out of my hand,*

*who is moving her jaws back and forth instead of up and down*

*who is gazing around with her enormous and complicated eyes.*

*Now she lifts her pale forearms and thoroughly washes her fac*

*Now she snaps her wings open, and floats away.*

*I don't know exactly what a prayer is.*

*I do know how to pay attention, how to fall down*

*into the grass, how to kneel in the grass,*

*how to be idle and blessed, how to stroll through the fields which is what I have been doing all day.*

*Tell me, what else should I have done?*

*Doesn't everything die at last, and too soon?*

*Tell me, what is it you plan to do*

*With your one wild and precious life?*

**Meditation and Mindfulness Practice:**

Sit with Mary Oliver's Poem and mindfully consider each line. Then go back to page 120 of this book and reread the Epilogue-A Call to Action.

**Self-Reflection:** How has this book and the journey you have taken changed you? Given these changes, tell me, what is it you plan to do with your one wild and precious life?

# Acknowledgments:

I would like to express my heartfelt gratitude to the many people who have played an indispensable role in my life and in the creation of this book. While I cannot mention everyone individually due to space constraints, please know that your influence on my life and this book is deeply appreciated.

To my beloved wife, Trish, your profound insights, and unwavering support were instrumental in enabling me to write this book. Your multiple readings of the manuscript and suggestions were essential. Our Saturday morning coffee conversations provided invaluable guidance, especially during my moments of frustration and confusion in the writing process.

To my incredible children and grandchild, Leah, Grace, Sarah, Candice, Adam, Rachel, Shane, Donna, and Josh, your love and support have been a constant source of inspiration. Josh, your contribution to Chapter 7 will have a profound impact on the readers, and I'm immensely grateful for your involvement.

Maureen, your counseling and guidance through the intricacies of my 'shadow' work were pivotal in helping me understand and convey the concepts of emotional healing and enhancing human (my) worthiness in this book. Your insights, suggestions, and feedback, especially with your background in Gestalt therapy, were invaluable.

Sofia, your timing in entering my life was unexpectedly wonderful. Your meticulous editing, multiple revisions, valuable suggestions, and the conception of the "Another Way with Dr. Ski and Sofia" podcast were and will be instrumental in bringing this book to the world.

To my precious friends at Artworks, your love, spirits, and hugs sustained me more than you will ever know throughout the writing process.

To the gracious people of Mexico, particularly in Puerto Penasco, who provided sustenance, support, and even prayers on the beach during moments of desperation, you were my special angels in this writing journey. Special thanks to Lillianna for your encouraging words and beautiful heart.

Glenn, your Sunday sermons, and friendship have been a profound source of inspiration and support.

A heartfelt thank you to the exceptional team at Authors on Mission, including Lindsay and Ava under the remarkable leadership of Vikrant. Your contributions were instrumental in making this book a reality.

The collective efforts of all these remarkable individuals have made this book possible, and for that, I am eternally grateful.

# About The Authors

## Dr. Ski Chilton Bio

Dr. Ski Chilton is a distinguished innovator, academic, and entrepreneur. With a prolific record of over 170 scientific publications and 15 patents, he has founded four companies and a nonprofit. He has been at the forefront of personalized nutrition and wellness, earning widespread recognition in both academia and industry for his trailblazing contributions.

In addition to his academic publications, Dr. Chilton has authored five lay books on physical and mental health. Particularly notable among these are *Inflammation Nation*, which foresaw the inflammation epidemic, and *The Rewired Brain*, which focused on the profound influence of the unconscious mind.

His list of awards is extensive. He received the Alumni Award for

Academic and Professional Achievement from Western Carolina University, and the Established Investigator Award from Wake Forest School of Medicine. More recently, the University of Arizona honored him with both the Outstanding Research Impact Award and the Inventor of the Year Award. He was also recently inducted into the prestigious National Academy of Inventors.

## Josh Chilton Bio

Josh Chilton is a passionate advocate for addiction recovery and a sought-after motivational speaker at treatment centers across the United States. He has been spotlighted in Hazelden Betty Ford's magazine "Better Together" and has made notable appearances on recovery-focused platforms such as the "Let's Talk" podcast with William C. Moyers.

Currently based in Tucson, Arizona, Josh is studying Law and Policy at the University of Arizona, further equipping himself to make a significant impact in the realm of addiction recovery and advocacy.

# Social Media

**TikTok:** @ anotherwaytohappiness

**Instagram:** anotherwaytohappiness

**Youtube:** @AnotherWayToHappiness

**Podcast:** Another Way with Dr. Ski and Sofia

**Facebook Fan Page:** Dr. Ski Chilton

**Website:** www.anotherwaytohappiness.com

# References:

1. Tolle E. (2004). *The power of now: a guide to spiritual enlightenment*. Namaste Publishing; New World Library.

2. Tolle, E. (2003). *Stillness speaks*. New World Library; Distributed to the trade by Publishers Group West.

3. Tolle E. (2005). *A new earth: awakening to your life's purpose*. Dutton/Penguin Group.

4. Evans, Jonathan St B. T. (2010). *Thinking twice: two minds in one brain*. Oxford University Press.

5. Chilton, F. H. (2016*). The rewired brain: free yourself of negative behaviors and release your best self.* Grand Rapids, Baker Books.

6. Plato. *(1943). Plato's The Republic*. New York: Books, Inc.

7. Chilton, F.H. and Tucker, L. (2006). *Inflammation Nation: The first clinically proven eating plan to end our nation's secret epidemic*. Atria Books.

8. *The Matrix*. (1999). Warner Bros.

9. Anthony De Mello. (1990). *Awareness: a De Mello spirituality conference in his own words*. Zondervan.

10. Lewis C. S. (1942). *The weight of glory*. Society for Promoting Christian Knowledge.

11. Catherine Liggett. (2023). *Holistic Mental Health Coaching*. www.catherineliggett.com

12. Hawkins D. R. (2013). *Letting go: the pathway of*

*surrender* (1st Hay House). Hay House

13. Fromm, E. (1941). *Escape from freedom.* Farrar & Rinehart.
14. Fromm, E. (19621956). *The art of loving*. New York, Harper Colophon Books.
15. Lewis, C. S. (1955). *The Screwtape Letters*. London: Collins
16. Hollis, J. (1993). *The middle passage: from misery to meaning in midlife.* Inner City Books.
17. Frankl, V. E. (1992). *Man's search for meaning: An introduction to logotherapy* (4th ed.) (I. Lasch, Trans.). Beacon Press.
18. Keating, T. (2014). *Reflections on the unknowable*. New York, Lantern Books.
19. Gould S. J. (1999*). Rocks of ages: science and religion in the fullness of life* (1st ed.). Ballantine Pub. Group.
20. Collins, F. S. (2007*). The language of God: a scientist presents evidence for belief.* 1st Free Press trade pbk. ed. New York, Free Press.
21. Schroeder, G. L. (2009). *God according to God: a physicist proves we've been wrong about God all along*. New York, NY, HarperOne.
22. Hawking, S. (1989). *A brief history of time*. Bantam Books.
23. Darwin, C. & Kebler, L. (1859) *On the origin of species by means of natural selection, or, The preservation of favoured races in the struggle for life*. London: J. Murray.
24. Darwin, C. (1871). *The descent of man, and selection in relation to sex, Vol. 1.* John Murray.
25. Jastrow, R. (1978). *God and the astronomers*. New York, Norton.
26. Dass, R. (20010601). *Still here: embracing aging, changing,*

*and dying*. Riverhead Books.

27. Lewis, C. S. 1. (2004). *The chronicles of Narnia*. New York, HarperCollinsPublishers.
28. Lewis C. S. (1960). *Mere Christianity* (Macmillan paperbacks). Macmillan.
29. Lewis, C. S. 1. (1989). *A grief observed.* San Francisco, Harper & Row.
30. De Mello, A. (1992). *The way to love: the last meditations of Anthony de Mello.* New York, Doubleday.
31. II Corinthians 5:17
32. Nhất Hạnh. (2007). *Living Buddha, living Christ.* 10th Anniversary Ed. New York, Riverhead Books.

# Endorsements

## Praise for *There is Another Way to Happiness*

As a physician, integrative oncologist, and New Age enthusiast, I have read hundreds of books in this genre. Yet, none have delivered a more pragmatic and accessible approach to living mindfully and joyfully. In his revolutionary book, Dr Chilton seamlessly distills concepts from groundbreaking thinkers such as Eckart Tolle, Carl Jung, and Jon Kabat Zinn in a narrative that is delightfully eloquent and profoundly inspiring. *There is Another Way to Happiness* is truly a beacon of hope and light, guiding readers toward a brighter, more conscious way of being. This will now be the first book that I recommend to my patients and anyone else on a quest for peace and happiness.

— Krisstina Gowin, DO, Associate Professor of Medicine, Founder/Director of the Integrative Medicine in Hematology Oncology Fellowship at the University of Arizona, and author of *Living Well with A Myeloproliferative Neoplasm*

Bestselling author Dr. Ski Chilton had a harrowing accident and faced death. This ordeal propelled him on a profound journey of self-discovery, during which he uncovered the true essence of human consciousness, leading to a remarkable healing of both body and mind. His inspiring narrative stands as a testament to the incredible capacity to transform pain into purpose. There is another BETTER way to happiness, one that lies within our own inner journey, and is profoundly illustrated within the pages of *There is Another Way to Happiness*.

— Anthony Atala, MD, Professor and Director at the Wake Forest Institute for Regenerative Medicine, with over 800 scientific publications, and a distinguished member of both the Institute of Medicine, the National Academies of Sciences and the National Academy of Inventors.

"Dr. Ski Chilton, a humane biochemist with notable accomplishments of scientific excellence and a previous author of informative books about human disease and health, now personalizes a quest for mindfulness and happiness—while applauding the wisdom of his diminutive grandmother. As hinted by the book's title, ingesting its content enlightens an ancient route toward happiness that never disappeared. This happiness route emerges for the reader from the 'sounds of silence' that whispers to Ski during treks with his dog into the canyons of Arizona. The name of the route is daily meditation. There are no toll booths."

— Charles (Cash) McCall, MD; Professor of Internal Medicine at Wake Forest University School of Medicine with over 250 scientific publications, former Director of the Wake Forest Institute of Translational Sciences.

Made in United States
Orlando, FL
25 January 2024

42899748R00148